Critical Conditions: Field Day Essays

Ireland after History

David Lloyd

CORK UNIVERSITY PRESS
in association with
FIELD DAY

First published in 1999 by
Cork University Press
Cork
Ireland

Reprinted 2006

British Library Cataloguing in Publication Data

A CIP catalogue record for this book is available from the British Library.

ISBN 1-85918-238-0

Typesetting by Red Barn Publishing, Skeagh, Skibbereen, Co. Cork
Printed by CPI Antony Rowe, Eastbourne

Ireland after History

CRITICAL CONDITIONS: FIELD DAY ESSAYS AND MONOGRAPHS

Edited by Seamus Deane

CONTENTS

ACKNOWLEDGEMENTS

Virtually all the essays in this collection have emerged from and been reshaped by conversation with friends and colleagues over the past few years. Several were first delivered as conference papers and benefited greatly from comments and questions in the course of those events. My thanks to the organizers of all these occasions. Some have also been previously published in other forms and I am grateful to the editors concerned for their suggestions and for the opportunity to receive feedback of a more anonymous kind.

The introduction was first delivered as a paper at New York University in December 1997, in a conference on 'Postcolonial Conditions: Ireland in a Comparative Context'.

'Nationalisms against the State' was delivered at several conferences before being published in a first version by Tadhg Foley, Lionel Pilkington, Seán Ryder and Elizabeth Tilley in *Gender and Colonialism* (Galway, 1995). I am also indebted to Walden Bello, Jackie Siapno and Eleanor Jaluague for inviting me to present it at the Forum on Philippine Alternatives, Berkeley, 1993, and subsequently publishing it in the proceedings of that conference. It is reprinted in *The Politics of Culture in the Shadow of Capital*, edited by Lisa Lowe and myself, and I am grateful to my friend and editor Ken Wissoker at Duke University Press for permission to reprint it here.

'Regarding Ireland in a Postcolonial Frame' was delivered at the 'Fighting Irish Studies' conference at the University of Notre Dame in 1995, and I am especially grateful to Spurgeon Thompson for his editorial help and comments as I turned the talk into an essay.

'True Stories' was first delivered at the University of Kentucky. Thanks to Jonathan Allison for inviting me there and for his generous feedback.

An earlier version of 'Outside History' appeared in *Subaltern Studies* IX. I am grateful to Dipesh Chakrabarty for his invitation to write this essay and for his editorial labours.

'The Recovery of Kitsch' was written for *Distant Relations*, a book catalogue for an exhibition of Chicano, Mexican and Irish artists. My thanks to Patricia Ziff, both for encouraging me to write this essay and for the magnificent project that she undertook.

The epilogue, 'Living in America', was originally written for the *Irish Reporter*, and my thanks are due to Harry Vince and Carol Coulter as well as to Ishmael Reed, who invited me to expand it for his volume of essays on multicultural America.

I have also benefited from the support of the Center for Cultural Studies at U.C. Santa Cruz, and the University of California Humanities Research Institute at Irvine, which enabled me to write several of the essays. My thanks to Jim Clifford, Mark Rose and Norma Alarcon for giving me these opportunities.

In bringing these essays together into book form, the support, friendship, unfailing intelligence, criticism and unmatched editorial skills of my research assistant, Greg Forter, have been indispensable: good speed in your new life, Greg, and thanks for many years of working together.

Through the years in which this book was written, Lisa Lowe gave me her companionship, the delights of thoughtful conversation, and the example of committed scholarship, all of which remain invaluable to me.

Numerous friends have contributed more than they may have realized through their comments and conversation over the last few years: Tadhg Foley, Lionel Pilkington, Kevin Barry, Angela Bourke, Carol Coulter, Clair Wills, Joe Cleary, Eithne Luibhéid, Aidan Wylde, Joe Lee, Laura Lyons, Bill Rolston, Denis Donoghue and Bob Scally of Ireland House. I'd also like to thank Mary Trew and others in the San Franciso Irish Film Society and the Free Roisín McAliskey Committee for their companionship and solidarity outside the academic world. Other friends and colleagues with perhaps less of an Irish connection have helped me over the years in thinking things through: Julio Ramos, Luz Mena, Paul Thomas, Dipesh Chakrabarty, Alfred Arteaga, Oscar Campomanes, Priscelina Legasto, Lulu Torres-Reyes, Leela Gandhi, Simon During, Ranu Samantrai, Judith Halberstam, Michael Davidson, Michael Bernstein, Rosemary George, George Lipsitz, Tak Fujitani and Lisa Yoneyama. My thanks above all to Luke Gibbons and Kevin Whelan, whose friendship, enthusiastic conversation, erudition and critical intelligence have sustained me, challenged me and kept me laughing. The best research was always done by ear. To my friend and editor, Seamus Deane, who invited me to bring these essays together for Field Day, my thanks and my regard for all the long work of building a different Irish Studies.

INTRODUCTION

> The current amazement that the things we are experiencing are 'still' possible in the twentieth century is not philosophical. This amazement is not the beginning of knowledge – unless it is the knowledge that the view of history which gives rise to it is untenable.
>
> Walter Benjamin

Reflecting on Irish culture and history, I find myself returning again and again to the insights Walter Benjamin gathered in his essay, 'Theses on the Philosophy of History'.[1] As with so much in the theses, this particular reflection is absolutely contemporary now: it is as relevant to our own shock at the 'recurrence of tribalism' or at the persistence of apparently outmoded cultural formations as it was to the disdain of Benjamin's 'historicist' prophets of progress for the foregone movements of the past. This book is concerned with the self-evidence of such amazement and with the forms of historical narrative that make that amazement seem so commonsensical. The essays gathered together here offer a critique of current historicism, which continues to adhere to the notion of progress or development and of civility at the expense of the alternative histories and cultures of which the story might be told. Indeed, as a number of the essays will suggest, it is precisely what Benjamin defines as historicism that not only relegates alternatives, past and present, to the condition of irrationality and backwardness, but *produces* them as such. Atavism is to civility as backwardness is to modernity, the necessary antithesis that defines by negation the proper forms and formations of civilized society. Historicism reduces the cultural forms and practices of past and subordinated people to mere reaction, folklore or mythology and yet depends on them for its own articulation and for its own myth of a finally triumphant progress. Within its frames, pasts that envisaged different futures are detached from any life to come, are fixed in their extinction, furnishing only debris, remnants, whose excavation proves only the inevitability of their passing, their fundamental incapacity to blend into the onward flow of history. However, on occasion, they may trouble history's stream with interference, eddies and counterflows.

That is why these essays attempt not only a critique, but a sketch also of possible alternative terms and methods through which to shatter and displace the common sense of historicism, the sedimented layer of concepts and assumptions on which its self-certainty rests. My title refers, of course, to our own moment, as post-cold war triumphalists proclaim the end of history and of ideological struggle and seek to reduce the whole globe by force to the mendacious triad of 'capitalism, freedom and democracy'. Ireland faces its own

1

forms of subjection to a New World Order that has long been in preparation. *Ireland after History* gestures towards other possibilities that have persisted outside the mainstream of developmental history, and suggests that they might be liberated from the regulatory force of an historical ideology that has governed political and economic decisions globally over the last two centuries.

That is not to say at all that *Ireland after History* pretends to furnish a sufficient methodology, or even adequate concepts, by which to construct a fully alternative historiography: that should be the work of many collaborators, from many different fields. What is collected here are strictly 'essays': trials, assays and sorties that seek to make connections, to find blockages and breaks, and, occasionally, to elaborate terms and relations that seem to tender space where the occluded can emerge. While, as essays, they respond to particular questions and specific audiences, they circulate almost obsessively around certain knots: historicism and subalternity; the state and colonialism or nationalism; the forms of representation, political and aesthetic; and, perhaps most importantly, the condition of what I have come to call non-modernity. For, throughout this collection, the endeavour is to find ways to speak about cultures, principally Irish, that are neither modern nor traditional, developed nor backward, but that occupy a space that is uncapturable by any such conceptual couples. The *non-modern* is a name for such a set of spaces that emerge out of kilter with modernity but none the less in a dynamic relation to it. It is, as several essays show, not the traditional, nor even, strictly speaking, the subaltern, but it is a space where the alternative survives, in the fullest sense of that word, not as a preserve, or an outside, but as an incommensurable set of cultural formations historically occluded from, yet never actually disengaged with, modernity.[2]

The lines of thought that are followed here emerge in large part from a longstanding concern with colonialism and, in particular, with its effects on colonized cultures. Such work inevitably demands a comparative approach drawing from the immense body of work – economic, historical and sociological, as well as cultural – that is and continually becomes available. Colonialism is an integrated phenomenon that operates across all the fields that in the West would constitute the public and the private, civil society and the state. No single event that occurs or institutional practice that is implemented is without effects across all the domains of colonized societies, not least because the aim of colonialism is the utter transformation of the colonized culture: the eradication of its structures of feeling, the subjection of the population to the colonizers' notions of legality and citizenship, and the displacement of indigenous forms of religion, labour, patriarchy and rule by those of colonial modernity. Again, colonialism is also a rationalizing endeavour that leads to the frequent replication of similar institutions and practices across the widely spread and diverse colonies of each imperial power. Not least, colonialism produces powerful and phantasmic ideologies that are no less fantastic for being woven and sustained through its quasi-scientific studies in racial typology, history and the economics of development. Nowhere more than under colonialism is the deep unreason of reason more compellingly in evidence.

Yet this representation of colonialism is merely a schematization of the norms and ends of a global process. Comparative work on colonialism's processes and effects draws out not only the ubiquity and replication of forms of colonial rule but also the remarkably diverse ways its rationalizing drive is deflected by the particularities of each colonized culture. There are no identical colonial situations, so that in place of comparative we should in fact employ the term 'differential', marking the ways in which quite specific cultural forms emerge in relation to a universalizing process. That relational moment within differential analysis is crucial, for the actual formation of colonial societies takes place precisely within the uneven encounter between a globalizing project founded in and still legitimated by Europe's delusion of universality and the multiple and different social imaginaries at work in colonized cultures. Without such a differential approach, the analysis of colonialism tends towards either bad abstraction or a positivistic catalogue of singularities and leads to a conceptual inanity within which the import of the singularity is permanently evanescent. Differential analysis, however, marks the rhythmic insistence of cultural singularities that emerge in relation to colonial structures, so that the study of one given site may be profoundly suggestive for the understanding of another, without the two sites having to display entire congruence. Throughout these essays I have tried to indicate how the insights and methods, not only of 'postcolonial theory' but of what I term postcolonial *projects* in the chapter 'Regarding Ireland in a Postcolonial Frame', help to reconceptualize Irish cultural processes and, no less, are themselves modified along the way.

Evidently, to introduce a collection of essays on Ireland with these reflections on colonialism and modernity is to insist that Ireland has indeed undergone colonialism and in part continues to do so. This assertion about Ireland's cultural and historical status continues to be contested and not surprisingly, given the political stakes involved. To assert that Ireland is and has been a colony is certainly to deny the legitimacy of British government in Northern Ireland and no less to question the state and governmental structures that have been institutionalized in the postcolonial Free State and Republic of Ireland. It is to demand that each state's claim to the monopoly of violence within their territories be rigorously thought through in light of their own very arbitrary and violent foundations. Such questioning does not, as many will be quick to charge, confer automatic legitimacy on any armed insurrectionary movement, movements all too simplistically and tendentiously termed terrorist. What it does demand, however, is that the phenomenon of violence must be understood as constitutive of social relations within the colonial capitalist state, whose practices institutionalize a violence which, though cumulative, daily and generally unspectacular, is normalized precisely by its long duration and chronic nature. Unlike insurgency, which is usually represented as sporadic and of the nature of a temporary 'crisis', the violence of the state operates through its institutions continuously, producing the material effects of poverty, unemployment, sickness, depopulation and emigration. That these phenomena are generally not seen as state-mediated effects of capitalist and colonial violence forces us to recognize that the violence of the state lies in its capacity to control representation, both political and cultural, thus regulating to a remarkable extent the 'common sense', in Antonio Gramsci's usage, of any given society.

The struggle over representation in every field of social practice accordingly becomes a crucial terrain. In the essays collected here, the problem of representation and occlusion is a constant preoccupation. The question of the past in Ireland informs the emergence of future possibilities, possibilities that are continually narrowed and occluded by a historical consciousness that seeks to write the complexities of Irish history into a narrative of modernization and the emergence of a well-regulated civil society. That narrative, which has been amplified in recent years by an uncritical and literally state-censored media, celebrates the passage from Ireland's domination by British colonial capital to its domination by and participation in the neo-colonial circuits of global capitalism. Those who have raised fundamental questions about the continuing consequences of Ireland's colonial past have largely been marginalized in public debate, just as those who have raised legitimate questions as to the repression of fundamental issues in the recent peace process have not only been marginalized and abused but, in some cases, like that of the family of Bernadette Devlin McAliskey, directly subjected to harassment and inhumane treatment by the state. The insistent disavowal of critical questions as to the alternative possibilities has enforced the occlusion not only of a vast historical repertoire of social imaginaries but also of critical analysis of the present. What would it mean not to commit Ireland's future to continuing capitalist colonialism, to the status of construction zone for the electronics industry with its so far concealed but no less disastrous effects on the environment and its labour force? What would it mean, not to disdain but to take seriously, the still-persistent recalcitrance of Irish cultural practices to the rhythms and social practices of capitalist modernity? What will it cost to resist not just British occupation and domination, but absorption into the immense injustice of transnational capital and the destructive logic of international military alliances? What does it in practice mean to project what Gerry Adams has called a non-sexist, non-sectarian and democratic Republic? Hegemonic resistance to addressing these questions is itself a symptom of the unfinished project of decolonization in Ireland and entirely fulfils Fanon's angry prognosis in *The Wretched of the Earth* that the future of the bourgeois post-colony was to become the conduit of neo-colonial capital.

The questions raised by Ireland's colonial status are pressing and intellectually profound. It is, therefore, unfortunate that so much of the objection to that claim has been intellectually vacuous, deploying *ad personam* vitriol and caricature rather than reasoned argument. The irrationality of such polemic bespeaks its embeddedness in anxiety and disavowal rather than rationally articulable positions, and more often than not it betrays its own astounding ignorance of the postcolonial work it reviles in its cartoons. There are, however, a number of effective arguments in circulation that seek to problematize or refute the claim that Ireland has undergone the historical experience of colonialism and may therefore be considered, at least in part, as a postcolonial nation. These essays in general insist that Ireland has never in fact had the status of a colony or that comparison with other countries considered postcolonial reveals only Ireland's vastly more developed social and economic condition. The force of these arguments obliges postcolonial critics to consider more thoroughly the legitimacy of our own claim that Ireland has been and continues to be colonized in distinct and materially significant ways. I want to address two essays that have had relatively wide circulation and which succinctly address the issues involved, but not in order to attempt a global refutation of these and related arguments, which would only extend a potentially endless round of empirical claims and counter-claims. It seems more valuable to focus on and clarify the methodological or theoretical differences that underlie our different interpretations of Irish history. The first of these is Thomas Bartlett's useful historical essay, "What Ish My Nation?"; the second is Liam Kennedy's more recent, economically based essay, 'Modern Ireland: Postcolonial Society or Postcolonial Pretensions'. I choose these two essays, not because they are the only arguments of their kind, but because each, historical and economic respectively, efficiently condenses the principal arguments made everywhere to refute Ireland's colonial history. Though they overlap at times in their concerns, I will engage each in turn to draw out a distinct theoretical critique of their disciplinary terms and deployment of concepts, a critique directed foremost at the limitations of empirical method.

The historical arguments against considering Ireland as a colony have yet to be better summarized than by Thomas Bartlett in his essay, ' "What Ish My Nation?": Themes in Irish History, 1550–1850'.[3] Though it must be said from the outset that Bartlett is not solely concerned with the colonial question and that his brief does not include the post-Famine era, in which the dissemination of nationalism is most extensive, his essay well exemplifies the kind of historical arguments that need to be adduced in order to call colonialist claims into question.

Bartlett's arguments are several. In the first place, though he acknowledges that during the late seventeenth and eighteenth centuries 'Ireland bears most, if not all, of the hallmarks of a colony',[4] he notes the fact that 'few Irishmen – Protestant or Catholic – accepted that Ireland was a colony with the attendant attributes of inferiority and subordination'.[5] The arguments made were generally for its rightful status as a separate kingdom. Secondly, 'unlike other colonies, Ireland was not located in some distant continent, nor did she supply the mother country with otherwise unobtainable raw materials or exotic products'.[6] Thirdly, given the massive emigration and transportation of Irish people to other colonies, such as Australia, Canada, Britain (*sic*) or the USA (*sic*), 'then surely Ireland, so far from being a colony, should be considered a mother country in her own right?'.[7]

These arguments are striking and embed a number of assumptions that are worth questioning. Of the third question, would it be enough to say that in some sense, then, South Asian communities in Britain, Singapore and the United States reconstitute India and Pakistan as 'mother' countries for their new states of citizenship, or Korean immigrants make Korea an American mother country? It is well known that the effects of foreign military and commercial interventions, from imperial commercial and territorial wars to extensive colonization, displace large segments of indigenous populations who are forced to migrate in order merely to survive. Most often, and especially when coerced, that emigration must be to locations either in the imperial nation or within its territories. More is obscured here, however, than aspects of comparative global history, the ignoring of which leads to an inaccurate positing of 'Irish exceptionalism'. This argument could not have been made without the apparent *whiteness* of the Irish emigrants, which seems to naturalize their later and complex identification with Ireland as a white European point of origin, and to obscure the massive differences in the meaning of emigration by positing destination rather than point of origin as the significant factor. That some Irish were in their turn to become colonists elsewhere, or to be instruments of colonial rule – as were the Senegalese troops or the Gurkhas, for example – says nothing as to the condition of the Ireland they were mostly obliged to leave. There, to a very large degree, they were not in fact considered to be racially identical with 'Anglo-Saxons' or other Europeans. On the contrary, their capacity to become colonizers involved, as many have now shown, a considerable labour of redefinition and of racist self-differentiation from the non-white populations of their new nations. The apparent whiteness of the Irish is accordingly a frequent casual objection to the idea of Ireland being a 'third world' or postcolonial nation. In fact, the doubt usually reveals to a considerable degree the anxiety 'white' subjects tend to feel in being identified with peoples of colour. What slips in here at the foundation of the argument is both the problematic history of racialization and a prior assumption, masked by the racial issue, as to the incomparability of the Irish experience to non-European ones. We will return to emigration more extensively in the context of Kennedy's essay, pausing here for some more general reflections on the concept of colonialism that Bartlett's work suggests.

What occurs in his essay is a common enough confusion of the distinct categories of colonization and of the subject positions within which colonialism is apprehended and, over time, conceptualized. There are distinct differences between colonization as exemplified in the colonial United States or Australia and colonization as a term used to describe the effects of French or

British imperialism and governance in North and West Africa. The 'colonial' period in US history refers in the first place, not to the colonization of the land and the subordination, displacement and extermination of its indigenous peoples, but to the relations between a white settler population and England as the dominant and regulative power. 'Independence' then refers not to the process of decolonization, as understood by indigenous populations, but to the establishment of an autonomous but no less European and imperial state form by the settlers. What for the settlers inaugurates, in anachronistic terms, a postcolonial era, inaugurates for the indigenous and slave populations a period of intensified and increasingly extended colonization. This example embodies two theoretical points: one is that the designations 'colonial' and 'postcolonial' involve not mere empirical judgement but the consideration of historical human subjects and their social relations as subjects and objects; the other is that the collapsing of the term 'colony' into a single set of characteristics ignores the gradual shifts and accumulations of meaning that mark it as a crucially temporal rather than an ideal concept.

Colonialism is, if I may put it so, always a forged concept, one whose significance is subject to iterations and reiterations that are predicated on materially embedded political and cultural struggles. It is, accordingly, more or less immaterial whether the 'Irish lawyers and politicians' of the eighteenth century argued for the status of a separate kingdom for Ireland or conceived of the country as a colony in the American sense. That is an historiographical move which at once privileges the perspective of élite classes and assumes already the historical development of a concept whose full range of meanings emerged gradually through the nineteenth and into the twentieth century. I would propose, instead, that we understand the designation colonial to be, in Marx's sense, a 'rational abstraction' rather than a transhistorical concept.[8] That is, it is a concept that can only function, like 'labour' and 'exchange', a posteriori, at the point when the phenomena it designates and unifies have emerged in their full material actuality. Thus, just as we can call barter a form of exchange only when the abstraction of 'exchange' as a distinct economic process has been made possible, so, for example, we can refer to India as a British colony only at the point where British governmental administration rather than East India Company mercantile practices dominates and the process of administrative rationalization occurs by way of metropolitan decisions and concerns: retrospectively, we can see the work of the East India Company as a phase of colonialism, though the word itself may not have been used. But the mid nineteenth-century emergence of the British state as governing power is definitive. Indeed, the function of the modern state is, virtually everywhere, critical to the definition of colonialism.

Most of the essays in *Ireland after History* circulate around the question of the state and state formation, its discursive self-legitimation and hegemonic institutions. They do so, however, not according to the 'revisionist' logic in which British rule involved the gradual extension of modern institutions into a backward society, but in relation to the 'failure of state-building', to borrow Ian Lustick's valuable term.[9] Like Algeria, which Lustick also discusses, Ireland becomes a 'colony' rather than a region of the state exactly where the extension of the British state finds its limit in the deep recalcitrance of Irish economic and cultural practices to 'modern' institutions and subject formation. Through the nineteenth century, this recalcitrance is increasingly understood as embedded in the Irish 'national character', or in racial difference, thus influencing the emergence of state policies that combine deliberate depopulation of the country with projects that entail the radical transformation of Irish subjectivities economically and culturally.[10] In turn, the emergence of nationalism in Ireland is no less shaped by racialized distinctions that have come to underlie the cultural and social projects of many nationalists. The intrinsic resistance of Irish ways to modernization thus inflects both the state's incorporative projects and nationalism's alternative conceptions of Ireland's future. An extended interface between modern and non-modern social formations arises that can best be understood in relation to other colonial sites. The first three essays in this book elaborate these processes more fully.

What I imply here about the texture of Irish and, by extension, colonial histories is that within them the characteristically distinct spheres of modernity – economic, political, legal, cultural, etc. – prove impossible to maintain. Furnishing in some cases an opportunity for nationalist mobilization, this lability of social space presents a profound problem for the colonial as for the postcolonial state. It is no less a problem for intellectual disciplines which define their distinct objects in relation to modern institutions and spheres of practice – economics, political science, sociology, art, etc. As we shall see further in this book, the disciplines depend on the stable location of a modern subject and develop their assumptions, whether political, economic, social or aesthetic, entirely within the terms of modernizing rationalities. The final aim of this rationality is the formation of a modern civil society alongside a developed economy; further entailed in it is the generally implicit assumption of an ethical, disinterested subject, disinterested by virtue of a prior formation and objective or truthful through submission to disciplinary norms. Hence the all-too-often unbalanced character of attacks on postcolonialism and cultural studies, or on the even more nebulous spectre of 'postmodernism'. In each case, though in quite different ways, these inter- or post-disciplinary intellectual tendencies challenge both the integrity of the disciplines and the self-evidence of civil society, and in doing so necessarily displace their ethical assumptions. The *moral* criticism of postcolonial work clearly precedes any intellectual engagement with it, since the ethical status of the disciplinary subject is *a priori* at stake. Hence it is possible for an economist like Liam Kennedy to infer 'postcolonial *pretensions*' with scarcely a single citation of any scholar or work and without extended engagement with any argument. The positivistic method that substantiates his own position is entirely in keeping with this *a priori* ethical judgement: Kennedy cannot attend to modes of argument that would question the objective validity of facts in abstraction.[11]

For the sake of brevity, I will focus on one exemplary set of statistics that Kennedy offers. The function of such tables is to demonstrate the irrefutability of facts and the validity of empirical comparative method: you cannot disagree with facts. The structuring of the data in a table simultaneously demands, as an unexamined methodological procedure, a remarkable degree of isolation and abstraction. Elements of a given social economy are excised from their differential relationship to historical processes and related formations and placed in comparison with equally isolated elements in a table that seeks to display a set of significant comparisons. What it actually displays is a set of partial relations organized according to a hierarchical axis that embodies unexamined values. Facts become entirely abstracted from the human agencies and acts that have constituted them in relation to a larger matrix of interdeterminant conditions. Kennedy's Table 1 [12] is a notable instance of the effects of such abstraction:

Economic structure: Share of the labour force (%) in agriculture and industry around the time of independence

Country	Agriculture	Industry
India (1950)	72%	10%
Ghana (1960)	68%	10%
Algeria (1954)	88%	5%
Ireland (1911)	43%	25%

I cite a few of the statistics from a somewhat longer table, but this is sufficient for the argument I wish to make here, since the purpose is to examine the effects of a method rather than the accumulation of statistics.

Kennedy's point is quite clear: statistics on the economic structures of 'self-evidently' third-world countries when compared to Ireland demonstrate that 'there is a marked discontinuity between the Irish and these other experiences'.[13] The proper measure for Ireland is rather 'the contemporary continental European countries'. Ireland cannot therefore be usefully regarded as a postcolonial nation. Comparisons with other European countries were, indeed, frequently made around the time from which these Irish statistics date and throughout the nationalist tradition, from Davis through Pearse and Connolly. Primarily, though, the references were made in order to show the discrepancy between Ireland and European countries of similar size, among which Belgium was most frequently cited. The point was the anomaly of Ireland's underdevelopment in relation to other small European nations and this fact was attributed usually to British rule. Ireland had, indeed, been systemically underdeveloped as a subordinate entity under British imperial capitalism, in much the sense that Frank Andre Gunder, and other Latin American theorists have developed.[14] That underdevelopment took place not so much by laissez-faire or mercantile policies of extraction but by means of deep state-driven policies of social and cultural transformation that had drastic consequences for the population. The formation of modern Ireland occurred through the exercise of constant coercion and violence, that nonetheless never achieved the integration and homogenization of Ireland that would have extinguished nationalist aspirations. The conditions of (under)development themselves produced Ireland's colonial relation to Britain.

The economic underdevelopment of Ireland took place through its role as supplier of agricultural products, processed and unprocessed, to a largely industrialized and militaristic Britain. The cycles of crisis in agriculture and agriculture-based industries are closely linked throughout the nineteenth and early twentieth centuries to the ebb and flow of British industrialization and military ventures throughout the Empire, the post-Napoleonic crisis after 1815 being an early and spectacular instance. Only the north-east escaped this pattern to some extent, being notably the only part of Ireland to undergo vigorous industrialization. *Pace* Kennedy, who thinks it 'an irrelevance'[15] that location is extremely significant to the terms of any colonial analysis: this was the region of Ireland in which the impact of settler colonialism had been most intense and which later maintained, as James Connolly and others frequently observed, its capitalist social relations through the discriminatory and quasi-racialized deployment of settler–native antagonism. The specific development of an industrial proletariat in north-east Ireland was largely predicated on colonial social relations and the systematic exclusion and underdevelopment of the recalcitrant native population on grounds of culture, ethnicity and religion. In other regions, industry relied principally on agricultural production which was steadily subjected to capitalist rationalization throughout the nineteenth century with an ever-increasing emphasis on grazing and on cash-crops, such as barley and hops for the brewing and distilling industries. The registration of many of these industries – such as, for instance, Guinness – in England is consistent with a persisting pattern of net capital outflow from Ireland, where relatively low levels of investment are returned with a correspondingly large proportion of capital extraction. This pattern has continued up to the present and shows no immediate prospect of amelioration.[16]

The point then is not that Ireland is or is not directly comparable to other 'third-world countries' on merely empirical/statistical bases. Such positivist assumptions are neither required nor predicted by postcolonial methods. What is at stake is the process by which facts are related and the geographic, economic and political conditions and the social contradictions out of which they emerged. Structurally, the relations between Ghana, India and Ireland within the British Empire are not entirely different, despite the apparent variation in relative labour statistics. Each colony emerged in relation to the extraction of resources and shows marked differentiation between urban and rural locations: the urban and usually coastal centres become entrepôts for colonial trade and processing industries, while the ruralized hinterlands become locations of raw materials or of artisanal goods whose specific value depends on their differentiation from mass-produced commodities. Each colony in turn becomes the market for finished goods that are imported from Britain. Beyond these general structural correspondences, however, the use of comparison gives way to the detailed and differential analysis that once more grounds the moment of abstraction in the complex and specific relations of geography, demography, history, racialization, culture, etc. One might say that this is precisely what differentiates the study of colonialism from the study of imperialism, which tended to emphasize the macro-economic flows of trade and industrial and financial capital rather than the specificities and dynamics of particular colonies.[17] In order to grasp the particularity of Ireland's or of any other country's experience within the larger economies of colonialism, economic or other data need to be posed in relation to the specific forms of rule or modes of cultural differentiation and so forth that have determined the actual texture of the society.

One major demographic, cultural and economic phenomenon that Kennedy's selection of statistics omits to include is emigration, a phenomenon that, where reincorporated into Irish figures, profoundly alters the interpretation of empirical evidence. Large-scale emigration has been a constant of Irish culture since at least the time of the Famine, to the extent that the population of Ireland has remained virtually stable for one hundred and fifty years. Emigration has had a disproportionate effect on the rural labouring classes, their decimation becoming a matter of policy in British administrative circles and among the landlords from the Famine on. But it has also held back the growth of an Irish working class and the formation of specifically Irish forms of class political struggle; it has contributed to the official conservatism of Irish culture and religion by permitting the continuing hegemony of large farmers and petty capitalists through to the late 1960s; it acts as a kind of numbed-out cultural trauma and emblem of economic hopelessness. At the same time, it has performed great service to the state as a social safety valve and as a means to mask the otherwise potentially devastating consequences of our neo-colonial status within the international and transnational moments of the capitalist world system.

We can re-examine Kennedy's statistics in the light shed upon them by the invocation of emigration as a major and anomalous feature of Ireland's colonial experience. Unlike most other colonial and postcolonial locations, emigration has been for Ireland a *programmatic* instrument of colonial rule and policing, and remained the enabling condition of postcolonial economic development for both de Valera's isolationist Free State and the later, modernizing states north and south of the border. To have achieved proportional effects in India, something like 400 million people would have had to have emigrated from the subcontinent since, say, the Indian Mutiny of 1857. The internal and global displacement of populations, like periodic genocide, has been a common experience of virtually all colonized peoples, but probably the only proportional analogue to the impact of emigration on Ireland would be the effects of the slave trade on West Africa at an earlier moment in capitalist modernity. This is not to assert direct comparison but to mark emigration as the distinctive form of disciplining that differentiates the Irish colonial experience from most others.

The degree to which, even, if not especially within colonial studies, this factor has been passed over and disconnected from other aspects of Ireland's internal history is a striking index of how much we take emigration for granted. If, for example, we consider the rates of emigration in the decades preceding 1911, the year from which Kennedy's statistics are drawn, we grasp a quite different set of relations than his analysis would suggest.[18]

Decade	Number of recorded emigrants
1871–80	542,703
1881–90	734,475
1891–1900	461,282
1901–10	485,461

In the four decades preceding the eve of independence, then, close on two and a quarter million Irish people had emigrated, skewing irrevocably the proportion of agricultural to industrial workers on which Kennedy relies for his sanguine view of the degree of economic development in Ireland at the time. For the most part, they did not leave for mere adventure and the promise of a new life; they left in order to survive the economic and cultural devastation that colonialism had inflicted; they left because there was no obvious alternative. Their leaving has left a wake that works continually in Irish culture. It can neither be softened into the contours of a cultural diaspora nor ignored for the sake of exaggerating Ireland's twentieth-century prosperity: both remain predicated on the as yet unceasing pattern of emigration that for some cushions the neo-colonial history of our present.

As I will suggest in the last chapters of this book, the political and cultural meaning of emigration survives its official erasure and economic use value, returning as the basis for active forms of global solidarity rather than for the empirical disciplining of such 'imagined communities'.[19] For the moment, let us simply note that, without emigration, the Irish economy in the twentieth century, in terms of large-scale immiseration, disparities of wealth, and social unrest, would probably compare more to the situation of Central American nations or the Philippines in the circuits of US capital and domination than to Spain or Greece on the edges of Europe. In their undialectical abstraction, Kennedy's figures ultimately conceal more than they reveal, not on account of any attempt to deceive, but as an index of the intrinsic inadequacy of empirical method deployed in abstraction from social relations as a whole.

As an alternative, postcolonial method is, nonetheless, not situated to offer a more complex but still empirical proof of Ireland's definitively colonial or postcolonial status. That it cannot do so is neither an index of intellectual or scholarly ineptitude nor evidence of some unethical indifference to reality. It is, rather, a consequence of the critique of empirical representation and the recovery of alternative conceptions that are at the core of most postcolonial and related work. In fact, arguments based on the acceptance of Ireland's colonial history have indeed shown a greater explanatory power and offered a more inclusive depiction of the dynamics of Irish society than have other approaches. They have not only shown the validity and value of the study of other colonial locations for understanding the general contours of Irish history, but have shown the ways in which administrators and their ideas circulated throughout the colonial network; they have demonstrated similar patterns of cultural and psychic formation across colonial settings; they have shown how methods and approaches developed in other locations prove effective in the analysis of Irish social and cultural phenomena. They will certainly continue to do so. There is, then, no lack of empirical data or methodological acumen here: the reasons for the intensity of the theoretical and interpretive debates lies elsewhere.

Of course, as I have already suggested, part of that intensity stems from the inevitably political implications of the claim that Ireland has been and continues to be a colonized nation. The counter-claims are no less politically interested. Both claims also exceed their immediately apparent object, the status of Northern Ireland and the legitimacy of republican, British, or loyalist military and political agendas. They deeply affect how the future history of Ireland will be determined, in terms of political arrangements, economic self-determination, gender relations, environmental issues and beyond. In that sense, each set of claims is distinctly performative, in that they at once repeat or reiterate apparently foundational statements and in doing so constitute institutionally effective realities.[20] The performative nature of scholarship cannot, however, be acknowledged within the framework of traditional disciplinary structures: their commitment to objects of knowledge abstracted into distinctive conceptual sets as the *a priori* of empirical method prevents reflection on the constitution of structures of knowing. This is the case not only for the social sciences but across literature and history as disciplines also. The methods of postcolonial projects, on the contrary, trace their genealogies from works that intervened deliberately in the structures of colonialist knowledge and critiqued the relations of domination embedded in apparently empirical utterances: the critique of empirical method has always been at one with the political nature of the intervention, acknowledging that the apparent self-evidence of empiricism is itself an effect of domination.[21]

Along with the necessarily interdisciplinary nature of postcolonial projects, this theoretical self-consciousness as to the production of knowledge has made their arguments often unrecognizable, in both senses of that word, within traditional disciplinary frameworks. Hence the attempt to resolve interpretive differences on empirical bases becomes merely contradictory. To try to elaborate the theoretical bases of the essays in this book in relation to the general field of colonial studies seems more fruitful. Work on colonialism derives its methods in some senses from the dialectics of colonialism itself, grasped as an historical project that is at once global in its aims and effects and absolutely specific in its practice. That specificity is determined by the largely unpredictable repercussions of local conditions and resistances on the reductive procedures of the state. The differential method, which I have already suggested to be the distinctive practice of postcolonial analysis, is in the first place required if one is to elaborate the dynamics of colonialism in its contrary tendencies towards homogenization and differentiation. But, as Stuart Hall has argued concerning the deployment of Gramsci's Marxist concepts on the rather different terrain of racial formation, it is no less the case that the differential method itself is dynamic: concepts and abstractions that we bring to bear from other theoretical work have constantly and self-consciously to undergo modification and sometimes transformation in relation to other sites.[22] Ireland proves to be a location in which the relationship between concepts and material history is productively vexed, leading to a high degree of non-reductive conceptual differentiation.

Both abstraction and differentiation operate as effects of capitalist colonialism at every level of the world system. Abstraction, as is well known, is itself a material requirement of capitalist exchange – it is not a merely theoretical algebra. But materially, in order to realize equivalence at the level of the global market, capitalism has always demanded the regulation and production of difference through state intervention. This process can be articulated through many instances and through various state polities. There are, to begin with, intricate variations in the practice of different imperial systems that depend in large part on the historical moment at which given nations gain imperial power and on the extent to which they reiterate or define themselves against the practices of other powers. The Spanish Empire, forged in a virtually pre-capitalist moment, failed to be the engine for primitive accumulation and capitalist development that it was for less powerful rivals like England and Holland. Its colonial social structures were correspondingly less affected by the exigencies of industrial capital and may have collapsed precisely because they proved unable to produce and reproduce a capitalist dynamic. The structures of the British Empire, bound up with the need for materials and markets in the nineteenth century, proved in turn less flexible than the neo-colonial structures adopted by the USA after 1898 in the Philippines and Latin America. Each represents, nonetheless, one moment within a larger, evolving system of colonial domination. Within individual imperial systems, differentiations are no less manifest. Although administrative needs led throughout the British Empire to the formation of a native intermediary class, the depth of the penetration of British culture varies widely from Ireland or the Caribbean through India to the virtual apartheid regimes of British Africa. The British system itself differs markedly in intent and institutional practice from the French extension of cultural citizenship through education throughout its empire, or from US attempts to control its colonies through education supplemented by media and commodity fetishism.

The transfer of practices from one imperial site to the other takes place equally at more discrete levels, in the circulation of officials and institutions from one sector to another of the imperial system. Charles Trevelyan is one such instance: after having had a shaping influence on the formation of British education in India in the late 1830s, he transferred the logic of subject transformation from Indian schools to the administration of the Famine in Ireland.[23] Brigadier Frank Kitson is a more contemporary example: as an officer in all of Britain's postwar attempts to contain anticolonial insurgency – in Malaya, Aden, Kenya and Cyprus – he developed the methods of low intensity warfare and counter-insurgency that have been deployed in turn in Northern Ireland.[24] In doing so he employed policing structures that in many cases had been modelled after the formation of the RIC in colonial Ireland in the early nineteenth century and replicated, with local modification, throughout the Empire. Each imperial system, within the larger global structures of colonialism, furnishes a complex space of incorporation and differentiation, of generalization and particularly, of circulation and localization, all of which demand of the analyst an attentive differential practice.

But if the emphasis falls on the differential practices of postcolonial projects, what remains for the function of the moment of comparison? Comparative work across the field of colonial studies operates in several ways: it can identify the transfer of administrative techniques, such as education or policing, from one colony to another; it can observe ways in which the structures of state rule produce similar modes of resistance in quite disparate cultural formations; it can aid in defining the ways in which the characteristics of the colonized are coded and addressed as a conceptual/metaphorical unity across colonial discourses and regions.[25] It can, of course, also be used to shed suspicion on the validity of claiming the specificity to colonialism of certain practices or phenomena, which is how both Bartlett and Kennedy use it. Another instructive example of this is Kevin Barry's essay, 'Critical Notes on Postcolonial Aesthetics', which claims that the organizational structures of Jacobite and agrarian movements in England strongly resemble those of agrarian movements in Ireland in the same period.[26] This is precisely the kind of instance in which the question of similarity has to be posed alongside the recognition of differentiation: though similarities certainly exist between movements that resist the extension of capital at the same historical moment, their signification may yet differ in their distinct contexts. The English movements, and their later mutation into the Luddites, certainly shared some tactical and symbolical forms with their Irish counterparts. But such forms of action in England were put down within the purview of longstanding legal interventions, ranging from arrest and trial to the reading of the Riot Act by local militia. No unprecedented legal means were impelled into being and the disturbances remained within the traditional purview of the law. In Ireland, on the contrary, actions were generally aimed at preserving rates of pay for agricultural labourers, controlling landlord improvements and the expansion of grazing: they took place almost entirely in relation to the ongoing rationalizing of agriculture. At the same time, they invoked a range of Celtic personae, often identified with actual persons, which marked the distinction between a native economic and aesthetic mode and a foreign one. Perhaps more significantly still, the British administration's response was to introduce an unprecedented national and armed constabulary to replace the older magistracy – a response which was otherwise, and later, introduced only in the colonies. For the administration, and in hindsight, it was clear that Irish agrarian disturbances signified quite differently than did Jacobism or Luddism and required the methods of coercion that signalled the status of the British as occupiers rather than as mere enforcers of customary law. The distinction between the specific significance of similar social movements in different contexts is clear, and crucial to the structure of analysis.

The dialectical relation of comparison and differentiation proposed here is not one that ends in either theoretical or social resolution. The product of comparative work between analyses of the processes of colonialism in various sites is, generally speaking, formal in nature. The study of historians of Indian, Philippine or Irish social relations leads to the observation of common processes of cultural formation whose ends are non-identical but share a similar 'negative dialectic', a staggering movement of swerve and differentiation which I elaborate throughout this book. Dipesh Chakrabarty's and Partha Chatterjee's work on modernization, KumKum Sangari and Sudesh Vaid's volume on the 'reconstitution of patriarchy' in India, or Reynaldo Ileto's work on banditry and religious movements in the Philippines, all resonate interestingly with the implications of work in Irish labour history, from James Connolly and William Ryan to Emmet O'Connor, or of Thomas Boylan and T. P. Foley on economics. Each shows how colonial social formations emerge in relation to modernity, always skewed in unpredictable ways that I have already suggested constitute the field of non-modernity.[27] This perpetual clinamen of the nonmodern issues in the unclosable dialectic between a constantly reiterated form and the particular content that it can neither predict nor incorporate.

This dialectic is in the first instance a problem of incommensurable temporalities: the time of development, which folds all human histories into the same scale as advanced or belated modalities of progress, is always awry to the alternative rhythms of the non-modern. Accordingly, though I have drawn on many disciplinary methods and objects throughout *Ireland after History*, my principal engagement has been with the critique of historiography. As I elaborate it in the chapters that follow, modern historiography, across a broad spectrum from conservative to Marxist, is embedded in the rationalities of modernity, in the notion of progress or development as emancipation. With differing degrees of self-reflection, historians narrate history as the history of its own end, in the reconciliation and resolution of contradiction, finding closure predominantly in an orderly civil society and reformed state or occasionally in post-revolutionary socialism. In either case, history is written from the perspective of and with the aim of producing a non-contradictory subject. In doing so, history constitutes and differentiates the developed and the undeveloped, the civil and the savage, the rational and the irrational, the orderly and the violent. Resolution is the containment by the state of the crises constantly produced by the power of these differentiations. The outside of the state and the outside of history are the same, determined as irrational: beyond the pale of each lies not only the unknown but what is strictly unknowable to them.

The task, however, is not merely the critique of the political and epistemological forms that make alternative modalities invisible, but the immensely difficult work that that critique prepares for, which is the attempt to construct an archaeology of the spaces and temporalities that have been occluded. That task is only fragmentarily performed in this book, and, on account of the negative dialectics of the non-modern, will doubtless remain a necessarily disjunctive and untotalizable venture. The chapter 'Nationalisms against the State' seeks to rethink the implicit prejudices of historiography in relation to actual processes of national liberation struggles, in Ireland and the Philippines, suggesting that non-statist activists have, in the course of struggle, effectively grasped the alternative possibilities embedded in non-modern cultural formations and their intersections. 'Regarding Ireland in a Postcolonial Frame' elaborates the logic of postcolonial projects that stem from that kind of realization, and elaborates some of the ways in which non-modern practices have unfolded in nineteenth-century Ireland and contemporary Northern Ireland. 'True Stories' continues to explore the Troubles, focusing on how the distinct domains of history and cinema share a tendency to project as myth what their genres cannot represent. At the limits of representation, the appeal to a hegemonic 'common sense' fails and in its place emerges a set of myths and stereotypes that bear little relation to the grain of non-modern popular practices, reducing them to irrationality and fanaticism. 'Outside Histories', originally written to introduce readers of the Indian journal *Subaltern Studies* to movements in Irish historiography, both examines the possibilities of the 'new histories' in Ireland and elaborates the concept of the 'subalternity effect', as this is derived from Antonio Gramsci through Ranajit Guha and Gayatri Spivak. The final chapters are more concerned with the question of migrant cultures and their potential political interventions in Ireland and in the USA. 'The Recovery of Kitsch' critiques the habitual dismissal of kitsch and the frequent identification of political art as kitsch. Instead, I argue that kitsch, often seen as embodying a primitive or degenerate aesthetic, in fact preserves a repertoire of political icons that is refunctioned in mural culture, documentary and other artefacts to mobilize the layered temporalities of resistant cultures. The epilogue, 'Living in America', dwells critically on the rhetoric of the Irish 'diaspora' and argues that in the notion of emigration lies a far more politicized vocabulary for describing the effects of the displacement of peoples by capitalism and colonialism. The term 'diaspora' aestheticizes the material conditions that lead to mass emigration and depoliticizes the relation of the emigrant both to contemporary Irish society and to other communities in migration, whether in the USA or in Ireland. To refocus our attention on emigration situates our own colonial history in relation to the expansion of transnational capitalism and calls for a critical resistance to its local and global impact on people everywhere.

Ireland after History is dedicated to the work of retrieving the different rhythms of historically marginalized cultures and to the alternative conceptions of culture and of social relations that account for their virtual occlusion from written history. But it is no less dedicated to imagining out of that different knowledge the alternative projects that will convert the damage of history into the terms for future survival. For, if the forms of social practice that lie athwart modernity's spate are the casualties of its deep unreason, they are no less the ongoing record of its inability to engorge everything. In this subaltern refusal to be incorporated, and this determination to imagine alternative ways of being, a different future finds its means.

NATIONALISMS AGAINST THE STATE

In the large and still-expanding corpus of theoretical and historical work on nationalism, a singular contradiction so persistently appears that it may be regarded as constitutive of the discourse. On the one hand, as writers like Ernest Gellner and Benedict Anderson have amply shown, nationalism is inconceivable except as a product of modernity. For Gellner, that modernity is defined in terms of what can be succinctly termed the new industrial state, and nationalism itself is 'inherent in a set of social conditions; and those conditions . . . are the conditions of our time'.[1] For Anderson, the 'imagined community' of the nation is predicated upon the emergence of print capitalism and concomitant notions of 'homogeneous empty time' which furnish the formal space of the novel and the newspaper, cultural forms in which the abstract simultaneity of the nation can be imagined.[2] For John Breuilly, a less well-known but, to my mind, equally valuable analyst of nationalism, the emphasis falls less on the economic than on the politically transformative nature of national mobilization.[3] At the same time, and often in the same works as acknowledge its modernity, nationalism is seen as the vehicle or the stimulus for the resurgence of atavistic or pre-modern feelings and practices, at best as a nostalgic hankering after irretrievable and probably figmentary modes of sociality, a futile protest against inevitable cultural modernity or economic transnationality. As Eric Hobsbawm puts it, 'the characteristic nationalist movements of the late twentieth century are essentially negative, or rather divisive . . . [They are mostly] rejections of modern modes of political organization, both national and supranational. Time and again they seem to be reactions of weakness and fear, attempts to erect barricades to keep at bay the forces of the modern world . . . '[4] Where Hobsbawm sees this as characteristic of contemporary nationalisms in the moment of their twilight, Tom Nairn, in a generally more sympathetic account, sees the tension between modernity and pre-modernity as a permanent structural feature of this 'modern Janus'.[5]

In the present moment, the disintegration of the former Soviet Union and of Yugoslavia has intensified the bad press that nationalism receives in liberal circles, usually in a simplified form of Hobsbawm's contentions. 'Negative' and 'divisive', nationalism inevitably gravitates from separatism to 'ethnic cleansing', driven by economic insecurity and the resurgence of irrational but immemorial hatreds. But the fact that the same arguments are used to slur the social movements that demand equity for racialized peoples of western

19

nations who have been the objects of US and European ethnic cleansing, segregation and discriminations leads us to a different genealogy. Focusing as it may now on the undeniably painful events in some parts of Eastern Europe and Central Asia, current Western anti-nationalism has deeper historical roots and remains ideologically and formally continuous with traditional and profoundly racialized metropolitan antagonism towards anti-colonial movements in the Third World. Indeed, emphasis on the *resurgence* of European and Islamic nationalisms in the former second world conveniently replicates the widely held idea that nationalism itself involves a resurgence of atavistic forces which civilization, in the form of the centralized state, has struggled to expunge or contain. The notion of the *return* of inter-tribal violence which structures so much of contemporary reportage, as it has structured the discourse on newly independent Africa, ignores the role of the state in restructuring and producing ethnic or tribal antagonism, as Frantz Fanon long ago perceived.[6] More importantly, it substantially dehistoricizes nationalism in its multiple varieties and contexts, reducing its complexities to the binary and recurrent form of atavism versus modernity. What I want to argue here is that those accounts of nationalism which are currently hegemonic in the West are locked into a singular narrative of modernity which is able neither to do historical justice to the complex articulation of nationalist struggles with other social movements nor, consequently, to envisage the progressive moment in nationalisms which, globally, are not resurgent but continuous, not fixated, but in transformation.[7]

The mutually conditioning relation between nationalism and modernity is generally located in the exigencies of political economy in the fullest understanding of that term. It is not only that nationalisms generally seek to control the deterritorializing flows of capitalist economies, whether externally imposed or internally emergent, but that they seek to do so in large part through the politicization of a population in quite specific ways. Nationalism in this sense is, as Gellner has argued, inseparable from the nation-*state* which constitutes its end:

> Not only is our definition of nationalism parasitic on a prior and assumed definition of the state: it also seems to be the case that nationalism emerges only in milieux in which the existence of the state is very much taken for granted.[8]

Far from being a defence of traditional modes of social organization, nationalist mobilization, according to such arguments, effects the transformation of traditional 'moral economies', to borrow E. P. Thompson's term, into modern political economies regulated by the state.[9] Simultaneously, the effect of this transformation is to produce the modern citizen-subject, the 'interchangeable' individual[10] of political economy, and the social institutions – law, schooling, police – that permit the integration of any nation into the world economic system. For Gellner, the decisive concept is industrialization and the nation-state its unavoidable manifestation.[11] The related term for Nairn is 'development', nationalism being seen as the product of an uneven interaction between developed and underdeveloped societies and as the means by which the underdeveloped seek to 'make up' the difference and establish economic and political equilibrium.[12] Nationalism is accordingly a transitional vehicle or detour on the way to the cosmopolitanism or socialism that are the proper end of history, for liberal and left thinkers respectively.

It is as a consequence of nationalism's historically transitional status in such views that its structure is marked by ambivalence, its modernity constantly intertwined with atavism. It is interesting to follow Nairn's argument here: in the absence of the institutions of modernity, the nationalist intelligentsia of a peripheral or underdeveloped region is obliged to mobilize the populace through appeal to cultural or ethnic identity posed as against modernity:

> All that there *was* was the people and peculiarities of the region: its inherited *ethnos*, speech, folklore, skin-colour, and so on. Nationalism works through *differentiae* like those because it has to. It is not necessarily democratic in outlook, but it is invariably populist. People are what it has to go on: in the archetypal situation of the really poor or 'under-developed' territory, it may be more or less all that nationalists have going for them. For kindred reasons, it has to function through highly rhetorical forms, through a sentimental culture sufficiently accessible to the lower strata now being called into battle. This is why a romantic culture quite remote from Enlightenment rationalism always went hand in hand with the spread of nationalism. The new middle-class intelligentsia of nationalism had to invite the masses into history; and the invitation had to be written in a language they understood.[13]

We will pass over momentarily the numerous questions begged by this passage in order to stress that its logic is that the progressive moment of nationalism is achieved '*by a certain sort of regression*':[14] 'In mobilizing its past in order to leap forward across this threshold, a society is like a man who has to call on all his inherited and (up to this point) largely unconscious powers to confront some inescapable challenge'.[15] In this light, 'the emergence of irrationality in modern history'[16] is virtually predictable, the return of an already partially unleashed repressed.

Nairn's argument is virtually impossible to reconcile with Gellner's equally forceful contention that, in keeping with its relatively recent and historically contingent emergence, 'nationalism does not have any very deep roots in the human psyche'.[17] This incompatibility highlights certain problematic passages in these 'modernist' accounts of nationalism which will force us to rethink their historical foundations. Either argument is consistent with the well-known 'romanticism' of nationalism. For it is true that nationalism frequently relies on 'invented traditions', cultural phenomena which can scarcely indeed be assumed to have 'deep roots' in the psyches of the intellectuals who produce them, even where they are derived from popular cultural resources. Nonetheless we can read Nairn's argument as attending to a forceful 'atavism effect' in nationalism which testifies to the psychic power of its cultural forms *at some level*. The appearance of a contradiction between these positions derives from the metaphorical slippage whereby that which is 'psychically *deep*' is identified with that which is historically anterior. But this is no occasional slippage: it is in fact intrinsic to the general historical form of the argument about modernity within which these accounts of nationalism take shape.

Let us pass to the historiographic critique by way of remarking that in neither of these accounts nor, for example, in Hobsbawm's, is adequate attention paid to the psychic impact of domination in the cultural and political dynamic through which the emergence and formation of nationalist movements take place. Yet if, as is generally acknowledged, and often regretted, what nationalism achieves is a *vertical* integration based on political solidarity against a common enemy, rather than a horizontal integration based on class antagonisms, it must equally be acknowledged that such solidarity is not based merely in ideological manipulation of the masses but to some extent at least in the common experience of domination. (I speak here, of course, of insurgent nationalisms, rather than those of the metropolitan powers for which vertical integration is achieved in an inverse relation to the exercise of domination.)[18]

The key term here is racism, alluded to so fleetingly in Nairn's list of cultural items as 'skin-colour', and it is instructive to turn to Fanon's brilliant analyses of the dynamic of nationalism and of the relationship between bourgeois intellectuals and the masses in 'Racism and Culture' and *The Wretched of the Earth*. For Fanon, the 'insufficiency' of the colonized intellectual or migrant worker is not so much the product of the underdevelopment of 'his' pre-industrial society of origins as of the racism by which its systematic underdevelopment is legitimated. The phenomenology of racism, experienced as an absolute limit to the modernizing narrative of assimilation, opens the way to a systematic comprehension of relations of domination.[19] At the same time, it leads to that 'plunge into the past' which is, for Fanon, the beginning of nationalism in the emerging intellectual's turn back to 'his' own culture to find another reflection, another human image. If that turn to the cultural past is in a strict sense fetishistic because it involves the desire for an image of wholeness to set against the mutilating experience of deracination and alienation, it is so not merely on account of the subjective sources of the desire. It is in the first place necessarily fetishistic because of what Fanon terms the 'sclerotization' of the colonized culture, the paralysis of a society whose previous, relatively autonomous paths of transformation have been blocked by colonialism. What the dispossessed intellectual turns to is fixed, archival and available for fetishistic recovery only in part, because of the intellectual's own relation to it; in large part, it is because that culture no longer exists except as an object of archaeological recovery. It is, indeed, strictly speaking 'fetishistic' in involving the disavowal of the intellectual's cultural mutilation by way of fixation on an apparent prior wholeness. Romantic fetishism is the property of the intelligentsia. But what this means is not that the colonized people itself is paralyzed in an unchanging pre-history of modernity, but rather that the people has moved on, is elsewhere. Damaged and dominated as it may be, denied or unwilling to have access to the modernity of the colonial state, the people, Fanon constantly insists, nonetheless inhabits an irreducibly contemporary space. In this space, and out of the resources of a hybrid, 'unevenly developed' culture that is neither traditional nor modern but contemporary, the means of resistance are constantly being invented.[20] It is to the contemporaneity of the people that the trajectory of the committed intellectual often unwittingly tends, passing beyond the fetishism that is an inevitable moment of emergent nationalism and yet the specular double of the colonialist's denomination of the colonized as 'the people without history'. What is at stake is not so much the somewhat redundant attempt 'to invite the masses into history',[21] as the form in which those 'masses' are addressed. What for Fanon distinguishes the 'sterile formalism'[22] of bourgeois nationalism from the inventiveness of popular democratic movements is the former's inability to recognize the contemporaneity of the people, its desire to refine them into modernity.

What is common to most Western accounts of nationalism, then, is that they take its 'bourgeois' forms at their word, so to speak. That is, even where the tenor of the argument may be generally antagonistic to nationalism as a political form, what remains historiographically of that form is its self-representation as superceding or subordinating other social movements. In this, historians effectively fail to challenge the fundamental philosophy of universal history which underwrites their inscription of nationalism into modernity: the particularism of national contents, potentially in contradiction with the universalism of modernity, is resumed in the *formal* congruence between national narratives of identity, produced for one people, and the narrative of identity that universal history projects for mankind in general. This potential terminus of nationalism in the cosmopolitanism of nations was certainly not lost on nineteenth-century European nationalists like Giuseppe Mazzini or Thomas Osborne Davis, even if it is more systematically expressed by Ernest Gellner.

Granting, if only implicitly, the assumption that nationalism supercedes or subordinates other modes of social organization – both those that are then termed 'proto-nationalist', like peasant movements, and those that are seen as counter-nationalist, like feminism or Marxism – historians misunderstand the continuing dynamic by which nationalism is formed in articulation or conjuncture with other social movements. We will return to that dynamic later, pausing here to note the double form in which nationalism's modernity is posed against the modes it supposedly supercedes. There is on the one hand the question of ends: where the nation-state is assumed as the proper end of historical processes, only one line of development can be seen as the properly historical in history. Accordingly, movements whose struggles precede chronologically or coincide with nationalism, but are not identical or entirely isomorphic with it, can only be seen as *proto*-nationalist. In this, Hobsbawm's account of 'popular proto-nationalism'[23] accords with works written more or less from within particular nationalist perspectives, such as Renato Constantino's *The Past Discovered*, on Philippine history, or Tom Garvin's *The Evolution of Irish Nationalist Politics*. For each, popular movements are absorbed into the historically progressive trajectory of nationalism, so that what is significant in them is the set of traits which lend themselves to national ends. Other traits, which may indeed be incompatible with nationalism, such as modes of organization and communication, and certain kinds of spiritualism, are relegated to the residual space of historical contingency. Here they constitute the nonsense, the irrepresentable of historiography. On the other hand, this relegation writes such popular movements out of history and into the mythopoeic space of arrested development and fixity vis-à-vis the forward movement of nationalism itself. It is, then, to the resources of this mythopoeic space that national culture is held to recur in its atavistic moments, while its historical modernity finds expression in the state form. The state is both the proper end of historical process and the eternal antagonist of contingency and myth.

Form and end of history, the nation-state in effect regulates what counts as history, and gives the law of historical verisimilitude which decides between the contingent and the significant. This law, and its foundational relation to a universal history predicated on ends and on the supercession of a prior, contingent history, is spelt out in Kant's celebrated essay, 'Idea of a Universal History on a Cosmo-political Plan':

> the very same course of incidents, which taken separately and individually would have seemed perplexed, incoherent, and lawless, yet viewed in their connexion and as the actions of the human *species* and not of independent beings, never fail to discover a steady and continuous though slow development of certain great dispositions of our nature.[24]

Universal history on these assumptions, which are curiously Aristotelian in their narratology, breaks down an age-old distinction between history, which is the chronicle of all that is proven possible merely by happening (the contingent), and the poetic, which is the narrative of what seems probable according to ends (the verisimilar). Universal history is, in the strict sense of the Third Critique, *aesthetic*, not only in this rotation from the axis of possibility to that of verisimilitude, from metonymy to metaphor, but more fundamentally in its absolute relation to ends, that through which the manifold finds form. The historical judgement of nationalism is accordingly always also an aesthetic one, predicated on the adequacy of any given nationalism to the state form which is the institutional embodiment of the end of humanity. But what that implies is that the negative judgement of nationalism, predicated on those aspects of it which tend towards particularity rather than universality ('negative, divisive'), must be seen not only in terms of the temporal schema – 'atavism versus modernity' – that is most apparent, but also in terms of a topology in which the space of the probable is divided from contingency. On the continuum of judgements, nationalism is either absorbed by the irrationality of its particularity as irredeemably antagonistic to the normative universality of the centre, or it is divided between a rational, centripetal core, which finds expression in the state, and an irrational, centrifugal periphery in which there is a constant struggle between destruction and reconstruction. It is clear enough how this topology both articulates a global disposition of power, within which the nationalisms of the centre evidently are never in question, and maps onto the temporal schema 'atavism/modernity' by which that disposition gains its legitimating self-evidence (verisimilitude). The discourse on nationalism, in other words, is saturated with the entwined logics of development and of core/periphery analysis that are at present globally hegemonic.

Antonio Gramsci's brief but invaluable notes on this relation between the form of dominant history ('the history of the ruling classes') and that of state formation are now well known, on account of the impetus they have given to the work of 'subaltern historiography' within which some of the most valuable recent critical discussion of nationalism has been conducted.[25] Gramsci still retains, however, the view that the history of the subaltern classes is only contingently 'episodic and fragmentary' and will achieve the unity dictated by major historiography at the point when those classes, in their turn, capture the state. He is still working within the model of a universal history which regulates the history of individual national blocks. It is rather to Walter Benjamin that we must turn for the theoretical suggestions on which an alternative materialist history of nationalism in its relation to other social movements might be based. In a particularly luminous moment of the 'Theses on the Philosophy of History', Benjamin remarks on the relation between what he terms 'historicism', which 'rightly culminates in universal history', and 'progress', by which we may understand that narrative of modernity which is always on the side of the victors as underlying social democratic theory and practice.[26] In this end-directed political historicism, Benjamin discerns the displacement of a more radical socialist tradition, in which looking to the past casts a redemptive eye on the succession of defeats and setbacks that litter that tradition's passage to the present. Its rallying cry, erased by social democracy, is 'Remember Blanqui!'[27]

Those of us who come from 'postcolonial' locations are probably all too familiar with the accusation that we are overly obsessed with the past. But in these reflections of Benjamin's, though they can easily be misread, there is no space for the nostalgia of which we may be accused. What he is exploring is the meaning of a materialist historiography whose interest lies in an understanding of social movements whose potential and formative effects have not been exhausted simply because they were not victorious. The 'fragmentary and episodic' form of their narratives becomes, in this reading, not a symptom of failure to totalize, but the sign of a possibly intrinsic resistance to totalization. 'They have retroactive force and will constantly call in question every victory, past and present, of the rulers'.[28] From the perspective of a modernist historiography, these are movements whose lines of force are interrupted, inconsequential, peripheral to the main line of historical development. They are the superceded and overlooked residues of history and, in that sense, do not even offer fruitful sites for atavism to dwell on. For, unlike the matter of atavism, which is usually assumed to be in some prehistorical relation to modernity, these residues are history's unassimilable. Their very forms are incommensurable with those of a statist historiography, so that it becomes questionable whether their peripheral status derives from their 'actual' failure to enter significantly into the course of history or from their incommensurability with its narrative modes.[29] The answer, of course, is both: the recalcitrance of such movements to state formation is bound up with modes of social organization, symbolic and rhetorical styles, or collective ends which are what have to be dissolved and recomposed for the imagination of the nation, in Anderson's sense, to take place. The imagination of the nation is both the form and the representational limit of history, properly speaking. By the same token, as Benjamin most clearly understood, the recovery of the 'subaltern' for materialist history, and therefore not only for the archives but for radical practice, is inseparable from the critique of historicism: 'The concept of the historical progress of mankind cannot be sundered from the concept of its progression through a homogeneous, empty time. A critique of the concept of such a progression must be the basis of any criticism of the concept of progress itself.'[30]

Such a critique, which fundamentally challenges not only the concept but the form of history as/of progress, does not simply dismiss nationalism but rather rearticulates it with those movements which it has sought to supercede and which are, in effect, its constitutive antagonists. We will return to some instances of this, and their theoretical consequences, shortly. What this critique at the same time entails is a rethinking of the location and the meaning of the 'irrational' in relation both to modernity and to the nation-state. The historicist view of the irrational is, as we have seen, mapped onto a temporal schema: forms marginalized with regard to the state are attached to the prehistory of the nation and become sites only attainable through regression.[31] And it is the temporal axis itself, structured along movements of progress and regress, that materialist history calls into question. In its place is posed a topological model of relations, which is not so much the core/periphery model discussed above as a map of movements and contiguities, conjunctions and incommensurabilities, wherein the irrational is located in/as those spaces of radical discontinuity with the rationale of developmental history. We might say that the irrational is located in the topological cusps as that which is unavailable to historical representation. But its relation to historical rationality is akin to that of unsanctioned to sanctioned violence in Benjamin's 'Critique of Violence': what the state fears in each is an alternative system of legality or rationality, rather than the unbridled and formless motion of force which has yet to be subordinated.[32] The 'irrational' appears as such through the very rationality of the state form whose homogenizing drive connects the apparent particularity of national identities to the greater homogeneity of universal history. At one level, reason of state needs and accepts the thought of the irrational as its primitive substrate, as that which was required to be developed. But what it cannot accept or accommodate is the irrational that its own rationality produces by virtue of the drive to identity and which in consequence persists in irreducible contemporaneity. Benjamin's materialism demands always the contemporaneity of the dead, the subterranean persistence of social forms that make no sense, for the sake of their recalcitrance to the morbid logic of identity.

Now without doubt the desire of nationalism is to saturate the field of subject formation so that, for every individual, the idea of nationality, of political citizenship, becomes the central organizing term in relation to which other possible modes of subjectification – class or gender, to cite only the most evident instances – are differentiated and subordinated. Ideological and strategic subordination can take place either in terms of tactical priority – the exigencies of the national struggle demand the temporary suspension of class or feminist concerns – or in terms of the pre-modern/modern dichotomy – peasant movements, for instance, involve modes of consciousness which predate and therefore hamper nationalist politicization. The fact, however, that hypostasization of national identity as the central term of subjectification does not cease with independence and is no less predominant in great power nationalisms indicates that strategic questions are not the sole determinants of the process of subordination. The logic of both modes of subordination can be derived from the centrality of the state formation that constitutes the end of nationalism. The challenge that both feminism and class politics present to nationalism is commensurate with the resistance that they must ultimately pose, ideologically and practically, to the state;[33] or, to reverse the terms, the power which nationalism has historically proven to have in containing alternative social movements of whatever kind may be derived from its intimate conjunction with the state. For it is a peculiarity of nationalism that of all modes of potentially counter-hegemonic formations none is more thoroughly reinforced or sanctioned by the formations it ostensibly opposes. As we have been seeing, the desire of nationalism for the state is congruent, for all the particularism of national identification, with the universalism of which, indeed, the nation-state is the local representative. The superordination of nationalism is accordingly predicated not on contingent requirements but on its intrinsic logic.

In practice, however, the dream of nationalism is contradicted. This is not a question of the internal contradictions with which nationalism is rife and which need no further elaboration here. It is rather to do with the fact that virtually all nationalist movements emerge in conjunction with other emancipatory movements, a conjunction determined by the intersection of the intensification of social dislocations which any transition to nationalism requires and the proliferation of 'modern' emancipatory discourses.[34] Conjunction, however, does not entail entire congruence or subordination in the first instance, so that the history of nationalist movements must be understood in terms of their constant inflection not only by conditions of struggle but by their interactions with allied but differently tending social movements. We may take two instances of such processes here: the Irish Independence struggle of 1916–22 and contemporary Marxist nationalism in the Philippines.

The social ferment that preceded the Easter Rising in 1916 and the subsequent Anglo-Irish war of 1919–22 issued from constantly shifting conjunctions among a broad ideological spectrum of social and political movements ranging from the racialist nationalism of Arthur Griffith to the republican socialism of James Connolly (whose writings remain among the most important essays in anti-colonial Marxism). The spectrum includes the pacifist feminism of Hannah Sheehy-Skeffington, the cultural nationalism of the Irish Literary Revival and Language Movement, and the socialist feminism of Constance Markievicz and, in her later years, Maud Gonne. To express things in this fashion, of course, minimizes the extent to which most of the principal figures of the period in fact circulated through all the major movements, and the extent to which at different moments particular groupings took the lead, whether in the socialist-led strike of 1913, in suffragist activism or in the nationalist uprising and War of Independence. Markievicz, who was deeply involved in all three movements, was constantly alert to their intersections. Margaret MacCurtain remarks suggestively on their conjunction:

> It is true as Countess Markievicz asserted . . . that three great movements were going on in Ireland those years, the national movement, the women's movement and the industrial one, yet as each converged on 1916 they moved at their own pace.[35]

Moving at different paces, these movements attend to a time determined not by a single end but by their distinct ends, only one of which could be subsumed in the declaration of independence of 1916 and the struggle for autonomous *state* institutions. Each movement has a distinct history and a distinct tempo which may be occluded but is not terminated by the consistent focus of subsequent history, nationalist or revisionist, on political institutions and state apparatuses.[36] But what is striking about their conjunction is its possibility: among the most radical nationalists were socialist feminists who clearly saw no contradiction between their distinct but articulated affiliations, though different historical conjunctures demanded different emphases. It is equally striking that these radical feminists, as MacCurtain points out,[37] unanimously opposed the compromise Free State that was established in 1922.

Markievicz's own political transitions are illuminating here. They are sketched out unprogrammatically in her letters from prison, written in several periods of incarceration between 1916, when she was arrested and sentenced to death for her leading role in the Rising, and 1923, when she was jailed for her republicanism by the Free State government. Certainly her initial understanding seems to have been that the nationalist struggle required the momentary subordination of the feminist and socialist struggle.[38] In her later writing, however, as the independence struggle progressed, her analysis of the relation between the history of colonialism in Ireland and the mode of the present struggle becomes closely tied to her understanding both of the requirements of socialist practice and those of the feminist struggle. The historical endurance of Irish resistance she attributed to the absence of a centralized state form, so that British colonialism had never been able to subdue Ireland through seizure of a seat of government or an acknowledged single leader. Markievicz proposes that, in domains ranging from language and education to political organization, Ireland's decentralization, though perpetuated by colonialism itself, furnished both the possibility for the kind of decentred guerrilla resistance then in progress and hinted towards the kind of social organization that might emerge from the struggle:

> There was something that prevented any man or woman ever desiring to conquer all Ireland – a sort of feeling for 'decentralization' (modern 'soviets') . . . It's very curious, for in a way it was that prevented the conquest of Ireland, till the English enemy got rid of every family of note: at the same time it always prevented the Irish getting together under one head for long enough to do more than win a battle. This makes me have such faith in the Republic. The country is now all organized and can do without leaders, but it has learnt that it must act together.[39]

Her antagonism to centralization and leadership emerges equally in her relation to the women's movement.[40] Throughout, the very articulation of distinct engagements together maintains all in a mutually critical condition of process, a process which the superordination of one reactionary version of nationalism in the Free State could only arrest.

It is not difficult to trace comparable conjunctions within the dynamics of the Philippine anti-colonial left since the mid-sixties, complicated perhaps by the emergence of a new left-influenced student movement and the neo-colonial nature of the Philippine state, which has been nominally independent since 1946. At least since the formation of the Communist Party of the Philippines and its break with the older PKP (Partida Kumunista ng Pilipinas) in the mid-sixties, leftist opposition has involved a series of shifting coalitions between Marxist and nationalist tendencies, student activism and longer-standing traditions of peasant and worker organization, guerrilla struggle in the form of the New People's Army and cultural work. More recently, movements for socialist democracy have emerged both within the National Democratic Front and outside it, as have feminist groups, including Gabriela within the NDF and Kalayaan, a feminist movement which co-ordinates across a broad left spectrum. The complexity, both historical and ideological, of the interaction of these tendencies is impossible to elaborate here, and I will focus on the conjunction between the CPP and rural activism, particularly in the domain of cultural politics.

The tradition of rural armed resistance to colonialism in the Philippines has been persistent if not quite unbroken at least since the 1840s, in opposition successively to Spanish, American and Japanese colonialism and, since 1946, to neo-colonial Philippine regimes. This period has seen several strictly nationalist and/or Marxist military struggles (most significantly, the nationalist struggle against the Spanish and then American forces from 1896 to 1902, led by the *ilustrado* élite, and the PKP-led campaign in the early 1950s). Yet it is clear that armed movements in the Philippines have never been entirely identifiable with 'modernist' political movements. In fact, stemming from a long tradition of what the Spanish first castigated as 'banditry', armed resistance has shown a capacity for persistence and survival beyond that of state-oriented movements whose ends have forced them into frontal offensives with superior imperial forces. Despite the 'legal murder' of Andres Bonifacio – the peasant leader of the populist Katipunan who was killed by *ilustrado* nationalists in 1897 – rural resistance against the subsequent American colonization continued through 1910, long after Emilio Aguinaldo, leader of the nationalist Philippine Army, surrendered in 1901. Traditions of armed resistance continued even after formal 'pacification', often in conjunction with the emergent socialist movement in the 1920s and 1930s. Accordingly, rural guerrilla struggle became the core of Philippine resistance to Japanese occupation in the form of the Hukbalahap (People's Army Against the Japanese), whose resistance to neo-colonialism continued into the post-war period and was only put down with great difficulty and atrocity by the Philippine and American forces. The capacity of the CPP/NPA to mobilize in conjunction with the legacy of such struggles, having learnt from the failure of the PKP's 'premature' offensive in the 1950s, has been a principal factor in their ability to maintain effective control of large portions of the Philippine countryside and to remain active in others.[41]

Despite relative success in military terms, it is clear that such a conjunction between a Maoist-inflected Marxist nationalist movement, founded by young urban intellectuals, and long-standing if 'local' traditions of resistance could not be sustained without continuous mutual modifications of quite fundamental kinds. This process of modification is already reinforced by the neo-colonial nature of the Philippines, combined with persisting feudal relations in CPP analysis. On the one hand, the struggle cannot be defined simply in nationalist, anti-colonial terms, since its end is the transformation rather than merely the capture of the state. On the other, the neo-colonial nature of the state defines the terrain of struggle as that of the nation and the kind of vertical as well as centralized integration of oppositional tendencies pursued by nationalism remains requisite. The process of 'conscientization' that is fundamental to the politicizing work of the CPP embodies this double requirement: it seeks first to produce a class consciousness in rural workers through the analysis of specific local concerns, and second to connect that local analysis to the larger national economic and political system. What this assumes is the necessity of transforming local consciousness into national class-consciousness, a process mediated by the pedagogical function of the movement activist. In this process, accordingly, the mobility of the student cadre[42] becomes not merely a practical asset but an expression of the structural relations of a dispersed *national* intellectual class, formed initially in keeping with the exigencies of the *national* state, and a localized proletariat. 'Conscientization', in principle, occupies the intersection between the spatial and temporal axes of political modernity, transforming the local into the national through the development of a more evolved consciousness.[43]

It is clear, however, that for many if not most activists the work of politicization involves a complex and reverse transformation of consciousness in the direction of localization rather than higher-level integration. From the learning of ethnic languages to the encounter with local cultural and political practices, the experience may be one which challenges the desire for integration from the centre and discovers the relative autonomy of local cultural inventiveness. A model for this transformation of theoretical and practical understanding can even be derived from CPP founder Amado Guerrero's innovative 'Specific Characteristics of Our People's War'. Commencing from Maoist precepts concerning guerrilla warfare, and focusing especially on the need to maintain centralized control, Guerrero reflects on the peculiarities of guerrilla struggle under the geographical conditions of the mountainous and forested Philippine archipelago, conditions which hamper where they do not prevent continuous communication between central command and local operations. Under such conditions, what must transpire is a reduction in central control and a corresponding increase in the relative autonomy of local units.[44] Though Guerrero's emphasis is on geographical conditions and on military organization, the essay has perhaps even richer implications for cultural politics, particularly since the geographical conditions, always an obstacle to communication and centralization, produce and are complicated further by cultural differences which are deeply resistant to homogenization: there are at least eighty distinct ethnic groups and languages across the 7,000 or so islands of the archipelago, and, beyond this frequently noted ethnic diversity, economic conditions and corresponding cultural differentiations are remarkably various. What these conditions entail for cultural workers is much more than refining a sampling of the local particularities for national struggle; they require an engagement in cultural and social analysis with a view to transformative engagement, one which involves often a transformation of cultural and political forms in the process.

Nowhere has this been more apparent than in the radical theatre movement which has emerged in the Philippines out of the conjoined work of NDF cultural workers and the radical Basic Christian Communities. This has been amply described by scholars and activists, and I wish here only to emphasize two characteristics of the movement.[45] In the first place, though initiated by either seminary-educated priests or university-educated student activists, the interactional principles of radical theatre, in many cases formed through the theoretical synthesis of Boal and Brecht, produce a theatre which is as decentred in its forms and emplotment as in its processes. Participation of local people in the enactment of dramas leads not simply to their interpellation into the matrices of established political analysis, but into the local invention of the terms of political and cultural analysis, terms which have in turn the effect of transforming the practice of urban or intellectual activists. In the second place, and perhaps with more radical effect in the long term, such theatre enacts the breakdown of developmental schema imposed from the centre. Just as radical cultural movements, as part of their dynamic, demand that priority be given to local analysis, so also local cultural forms cease to be seen as atavistic survivals of primordial cultures and are rediscovered as functioning resources in their irreducible contemporaneity. The extraordinary syncretism of theatrical productions by PETA (the Philippine Educational Theatre Association), the umbrella group for radical theatre movements, indicates the potential for a performance that enacts the contemporaneity of multiple cultural forms in the name of a radical affirmation of difference against homogeneity. Peking Opera combines with Islamic dance forms from Mindanao or traditional martial arts from Luzon, as well as with Brechtian tableau or Spanish-derived theatrical modes like *zarzuela* and *moro-moro*, or similar religious ritual forms. In some respects, the theatre movement may be valuably conceived as a contemporary version of what Reynaldo Ileto so movingly describes in *Pasyon and Revolution* as the popular adaptation and transformation of familiar and hegemonically intended Spanish liturgical forms.[46]

Intense resistance to Ileto's work from some quarters, however, is a reminder that what is described above can only be thought of as a tendency rather than some achieved ideal. The resistance is expressed in terms of the antagonism between Marxist–nationalist modes of enlightenment and the 'primitive' superstition of the millenarian movements he describes.[47] Much is legitimately at stake here in terms of the exigencies of political practice, and the conjunctions in play are by definition in process. Nor can it simply be said that the radical theatre movement is unambivalently an agent either of conscientization or of more localized and syncretic processes: as a site of conjunction it is evidently also a site of contestations. Among the issues at stake in such a contestation is the relationship within left nationalism between 'modernity' and what we may call this 'contemporaneity of the non-modern', of that which has generally been relegated to the domain of the atavistic or irrational.

Two observations follow from these historical examples. The first is that it is the superordination of the state form that puts an end to the processes of articulation and conjuncture that maintain nationalism differentially as an element of broader, more complex, and often internally antagonistic social formations. This can take the form either of the actual attainment of formal independence or, at the ideological level, before or after independence, of the effective dominance of state-oriented tendencies within hegemonic groups or parties. The distinction is logical only: in actual practice, the independent state tends to be structured in accord with the ideology of hegemonic élites created by colonialism. Fanon's *Wretched of the Earth* is a relentless analysis of both aspects of this process. The fact that Irish socialist feminists could play leading roles within the nationalist struggle and be entirely opposed to the Free State that resulted is not only logical but may even be quite typical of decolonization processes generally. The second observation, which follows from the first, is that it is important to recognize that other social movements are not necessarily entirely absorbed or otherwise dissolved in the hegemony of state-oriented nationalisms. On the contrary, they persist as distinct elements of the struggle or as recalcitrant tendencies for the state. But they do so, not as particles of the pre-history of nationalism awaiting absorption, but as active constituents of the modern, inflected just as is nationalism by recent history, though with different ends and correspondingly different narratives. And these are continuing narratives: the fetishization of 'folk-culture' as a fixed and primordial expression of a transcendental people is in fact most often an *idée fixe* of official state culture, deployed in the monumental rituals and ceremonies which perform the identity of citizen and state. Popular culture continues its hybrid and partially self-transforming, partially subordinated existence in the shadow of the state.[48] Indeed, it is a paradox of nationalism that though it may often summon into being a 'people' which is to form and subtend the nation-state, it is always confronted with that people as a potentially disruptive *excess* over the nation and its state.

It would be wrong to see that excess as the index of irrational or atavistic forces escaping the controlling, 'repressive-tolerant' vigilance of the modern and rational state. What is in play, rather, is a chiasmatic relation between the designations 'rational' and 'irrational' through terrains whose specularity is staked out in the continuing contestation between incommensurable modes of subject formation or interpellation. If nationalism calls forth a people for the nation-state, its modes of subjectification still cannot exhaust the identifications available to the individuals thus summoned. Faced with that strictly uncontainable excess, the state designates it immoral, irrational, primitive or criminal. Yet the state in its turn depends on the mobilization, at the individual and the mass level, of forces we might term 'irrational', and it is exactly in proportion to the power of our own intellectual discipline that we fail to acknowledge the perception of the colonized or the subaltern that the state is crazy. As Theodor Adorno puts it in *Negative Dialectics*:

> After feudalism perished, a precarious form of centralized organization was to tame the diffuse combines of nature so as to protect bourgeois interests. It was bound to become a fetish unto itself; there was no other way it might have integrated the individuals, whose economic need of that form of organization is as great as its incessant rape of them. And where the nation failed to accomplish the union that is the prerequisite of a self-emancipating bourgeois society – in Germany, that is – its concept becomes overvalued and destructive. To take in the *gentes*, the concept of the nation mobilizes additional regressive memories of its archaic root.[49]

Adorno's remarks are in part founded in the analysis of fascism but recognize it as the extreme case of processes which are entirely congruent with the universal requirements of modern state formation. And if fascism recurs in critiques of nationalism as the horizon on which its tendencies are realized, we need to understand that this is in fact not simply because of the force of irrationality it unleashes, but precisely in the profound rationality of its unreason, in the violence of the state which is, in a formalist sense, 'typical'.

As is well known, the emergence of the modern state is inseparable from a massive restructuring of the modes of interpellation by which individuals are transformed into citizen-subjects who will, as Althusser puts it, 'work by themselves',[50] whether in economic, legal, political or cultural domains. Althusser's critique of ideology as determined by the category of the subject draws on a psychoanalytic narrative of the formation of the subject through oedipalization and its sublimation in relation to the figure of the father, the Lacanian 'Name-of-the-father'. The importance of Althusser's intervention in the psychoanalytic understanding of subject formation is, in a certain sense, belied by his own slippage into positing the ideological as universal and transhistorical. For where both Freudian and Lacanian paradigms can be critiqued for universalizing the decisive moments in their narratives, castration anxiety and the bourgeois family for Freud, the phallus as signifier of differentiation for Lacan, Althusser emphasizes the crucial historical importance of educational apparatuses. The meaning of oedipalization, as a psychic process determined by the specific historical form of the bourgeois family, can only be grasped in relation to its function within educational institutions against which the modern family is differentiated and defined. The pedagogical process replicates and normativizes the proto-ethical narrative which occurs, or is supposed to occur, at the 'private' level of the family. The disciplining of the individual subject, which takes place by way of what that subject learns to desire, paves the way for the socialization of the subject in accord with the ethical maxim of learning to will one's own subordination.

Insisting on the historicity of these social forms in no way diminishes or rationalizes away the psychic hold they exert upon the modern subject. On the contrary, Gellner's account of subject-formation in nationalism, which is remarkably congruent with Althusser's in its emphasis on education, implies a deeply disturbing psychic force which he sublimates manfully into an elegant historical joke:

> A man's education is by far his most precious investment, and in effect confers his identity on him. Modern man is not loyal to a monarch or a land or a faith, whatever he may say, but to a culture. And he is, generally speaking, gelded. The Mamluk condition has become universal. No important links bind him to a kin group; nor do they stand between him and a wide, anonymous community of culture.
>
> We are all of us now castrated, and pitifully trustworthy. The state can trust us, all in all, to do our duty, and need not turn us into eunuchs, priests, slaves, or Mamluks first.[51]

Gellner brings out here luminously, and with a fatalistic homosociality, the way in which what Freud first described as 'sublimation' involves not only 'the dissolution of the oedipus complex' but also that of the family for the individual, insofar as the *figuration* of the father as super-ego makes that figure available for transference onto other and generally abstract forms of authority. (By the same token, it is crucial for Lacan that the signifier of difference is the *phallus*, not the anatomical organ, the penis.) But the congruence of Gellner's own modernizing narrative with the forms he invokes and sublimates into metaphor prevents him from acknowledging fully their continuing irrational dimension.

This is neither to suggest that castration anxiety or the oedipus complex are irrationalities which are superceded by access to enlightened culture nor even to claim that the 'irrationality' of the state lies in its dependence for interpellation on 'regressive' psychic identifications. On the contrary, it is to take seriously the psychoanalytic contention that what occurs in these processes, at every level, is the constitution itself of rationality and irrationality, sense and non-sense. The sense of the state depends on the relegation of other modes of sociality to the domain of non-sense; its rationality requires the production of irrationality as the form of that which *must* exceed its modes of interpellation. Oedipalization, at the level of the individual, constructs obsessively that individual's sense of verisimilitude, but always obsessively precisely because, although it has the form of the truth, the ethical subject can by its constitution never represent the 'whole truth'. There is accordingly a link far profounder than Gellner can admit between the Weberian definition of the state as possessing a 'monopoly of violence' and his own revision of that to emphasize, rightly, the state's 'monopoly of education'.[52] The state must expunge, through ideological or repressive state apparatuses, cultural or social forms which are in excess of its own rationality and whose own rationale is other to its own. Though this may take the form of outright repression, the mechanisms of the modern state tend rather towards transformation (rather than transcendence) of alternative forms. Herein lies the secret and function of the fetishism of the state which invokes 'traditional' figures precisely to mask difference and excess. To take one signal example, the figure of Kathleen Ní Houlihan, often regarded by Irish revisionists as an atavistic female figure who mobilizes an irrational and regressive nationalism's devotion to oedipal emotions, is in fact a product of modernity and its insistence on the homogenization of national identity. Based indeed on popular figures, which, in the metonymic manner of popular/non-modern culture, made no hard and fast distinctions between the actual and the figurative, it reduces them to a metaphor for national identity and a powerful interpellative figure in the nationalist struggle for the state. It refines out of the popular, with its excess and overdetermination, an image around which to form the desire of political subjects. Nor is this a peculiarity of anti-colonial nationalisms: quite similar and even more fraught transformations are evident in the invention of France's Marianne after 1848.[53]

The modern state, then, is always in a profoundly ambivalent relation to the forces of rationality and irrationality at whose interface it is constituted. The displacement of irrationality onto nationalisms is an ideological convenience of a historical moment in which a further effort of homogenizing rationalization is taking place globally in the name of the New World Order. At such a moment, when the violence of nationalist and patriarchal states is literally beyond reason, and when that irrationality is conjoined with the profound economic rationality of transnational capitalism, there are sound pragmatic reasons to adhere to nationalism as a minimal defence against homogenization. But if the nationalisms with which we are in solidarity are to be emancipatory, rather than fixed in the repressive apparatuses of state formations, it is their conjunctural relation to other social movements that needs to be emphasized and furthered, at both theoretical and practical levels. The possibility of nationalism against the state lies in the recognition of the excess of the people over the nation, and in the understanding that it is, beyond itself, within the very logic of nationalism as a political phenomenon to open and mobilize alternative formations.

REGARDING IRELAND IN A POSTCOLONIAL FRAME[1]

The most interesting work in Irish cultural studies of the past few years has been charged with the double task of rethinking the legacy of the Irish anti-colonial struggles, in terms of their historical multiplicity and in the light of contemporary struggles, and of re-envisioning what have been too simply understood as nationalist movements in relation to a range of other unfolding social movements and processes. That these movements – agrarian movements, women's movements, labour movements, to name only a few – have largely been occluded by the dominant forms and debates of Irish history is an effect of the organizing concerns of official history: the formation of the nation and of the state; the narrative of political institutions and state apparatuses; in short, the modernization of Ireland. Accordingly, the very social processes, the continual transformations that take place not only within the purview of the state and the political sphere but also in its shadow, have been obscured, while the movements that have emerged from those spaces have been subordinated. It follows from this that any archaeology of those spaces and of the specific social processes that emerge in them requires not merely, at the empirical level, new and supplementary histories of what has been left out of Irish history, but also a more critical understanding of the forms of historiography that have shaped dominant representations of what constitutes the 'self-evidently' canonical matter of 'modern Ireland'. What is required, in every domain of Irish cultural studies, is a series of challenges to what is established as the common sense of both academic and public discourse: to their procedures, to their periodizations, to their hierarchies of identities and institutions, to their disposition of the local and the central, the traditional and the modern, the margin and the mainstream. Challenges, in other words, to the reasons of state that are embedded in the rationalities of history. This is not simply a critical project but, through critique, seeks to expand the space for the imagination and realization of alternative social forms.

In this chapter, I want to explore further the theoretical resources that Irish cultural studies have recently drawn and can continue to draw from their association with the extensive work that has been done under the rubric of postcolonial theory. This is not at all to suggest that postcolonialism should be the privileged term for Irish studies: there is, for example, an urgent need for a more extensive history of gender formations in Ireland, a task that would in any case be indispensable to and indissociable from the history of colonial institutions. We can, however, draw much from an informed understanding of the kinds of questions and projects postcolonial studies have helped to inform, and maintain the view that Ireland continues to be a crucial site for the understanding of processes of colonization and decolonization. We need to continue to be open to the suggestiveness of projects that have explored quite other domains than Irish history and culture, and to be attentive to the differences that our anomalous geographical and historical locations have produced.[2]

I will emphasize here the importance of postcolonial *projects* as opposed to postcolonial theory or 'postcoloniality'. In doing so, I want to distinguish the notion of a multiplicity of archaeological projects connected by a common critique of dominant historiography from the rather phantasmic notion of a homogeneous and homogenizing 'postcolonial theory' against which, of late, so much antagonistic energy has been expended. In the first place, I want to explore in what follows some common elements that inform postcolonial projects and constitute the possibility of linking otherwise rather disparate projects; in the second, I want to elaborate two concepts that have been associated with postcolonial theory, mostly through the work of Homi Bhabha – the concepts of hybridity and temporality. But I want to do this specifically in relation to the dynamics of colonialism in Ireland in order to examine how we might need to reinflect such concepts for our purposes.

It is with the status of temporality in postcolonial theory that I want to commence, since it seems to me important to designate clearly what the usage involves. In a thoughtful and helpful critique of the usages of 'postcolonialism', Anne McClintock has argued that:

> the term 'post-colonial' . . . is haunted by the very figure of linear 'development' that it sets out to dismantle. Metaphorically, the term 'post-colonialism' marks history as a series of stages along an epochal road from 'the precolonial' to 'the colonial' to 'the post-colonial' – an unbidden, if disavowed, commitment to linear time and the idea of 'development'.[3]

I would suggest, to the contrary, that this peculiar but not atypical reification of the *term* as theoretical agent misrecognizes the actual *projects* of postcolonial critics. By and large, refusing to occupy a position outside of historical processes, postcolonial critics and historians have sought instead to effect a fold in developmental historiography such that the multiple histories of social practices and cultural formations that were strictly irrepresentable within its terms might re-emerge from the cusp of their occlusion. Hence, of course, the continual intersection of much postcolonial work with the projects of subaltern historiography and related new histories elsewhere: they share a common concern with the social formations obscured by the implicitly developmental élite historiographies of imperialism, bourgeois nationalism and some modes of Marxism. This concern in part explains the infrequently noted phenomenon that a theoretical tendency designated *post-*

colonial has so often taken its materials from the period of colonization itself: what is at stake is the archaeology of alternative or subaltern forms of resistance which were in play alongside nationalist anti-colonialism, a set of projects which bears significantly on counter-hegemonic practices now, whether in the remaining colonized domains or within postcolonial states. Accordingly, far from inaugurating 'an entranced suspension of history',[4] such projects engage with the multiple temporalities that constitute the uneven fields of anti-colonial resistance and decolonization.

Let me exemplify this by returning to the observations by Margaret Mac-Curtain that were cited in the previous chapter. What I take her comment to imply is that to each of the different movements mentioned by Markievicz there belongs a different temporality or rhythm, defined neither by 1916 itself nor by any 'lag' in relation to it, but by the ends that define each movement. That is to say, if the labour movement is directed towards the ending of exploitation, if the end of the suffrage movement is the end of the oppression of women, and if the object of the nationalist movement is the seizure of the state, clearly only one of these is defined primarily by the goals of the 1916 uprising. 1916 is not the climactic moment for feminism or socialism that it is for nationalism, however symbolically. Now we know, of course, that each of these movements and others in fact 'converged' on 1916 and are only analytically separable from one another historically. But what interests me in MacCurtain's phrasing is the acknowledgement of the multiple temporalities that are involved in any moment of insurgence, the convergence of different movements around different ends across the same temporal frame. What followed in 1922, with the founding of the so-called Free State, is that that dynamic of convergence was superseded almost entirely by the superordination of a narrow version of the nationalist project, by the establishment of a conservative national state, to the detriment of both the feminist and the labour movements. Yet I would want to suggest that in fact at no moment in the longer course of Irish history – or indeed in virtually any colonial history – are such movements merely arrested. They are, rather, occluded, and fall under the shadow of the new state for, we might say, a moment of hesitation within the course of the struggle. They fall out of visibility or out of representation, which does not mean that they have been successfully truncated or arrested.

There are two modes of occlusion that I want to address here, insofar as they constitute objects of postcolonial projects. The first of these is the marginality that accrues to such movements in relation to official culture. As is well known, after 1925 the labour movement rapidly became a quite minor political force in Ireland, for reasons whose initial dynamic Emmet O'Connor has valuably explored in his *Syndicalism in Ireland*.[5] By the same token, the progressive aspects of the women's movement were increasingly marginalized, obscuring the radicalism of women like Hanna Sheehy-Skeffington, Helena Moloney or Maud Gonne, who were also involved in different ways in the national struggle.[6] The occlusion of these movements has to do with their diminishing access to the organs and institutions of civil and political society. But the second mode of occlusion occurs within historiography. One is continually struck in reading standard histories of modern Ireland by how little attention is paid to the importance of feminism in the national struggle or to the significance of the links between republicanism and suffrage. More importantly, only relatively recently have feminist historians begun to trace the alternative domains in which women were engaged as social and political agents, domains which cannot be subsumed simply within the history of the emerging nation. By the same token, it has been the work of a handful of historians like Emmet O'Connor and Desmond Greaves to explore the dynamics of the labour movement beyond its intersection with the 'larger history' of the nationalist movement. These are not the concerns of the canonical histories of Ireland whose concentration on the narrative of the nation and the state spells the close conjunction between the disciplinary formation of history and the institutional legitimation of the modern state. The work of postcolonial projects is to split apart the conjunction between the nation-state and its history, opening space for the recovery and articulation of alternative narratives.[7]

Accordingly, if there does appear to be a 'staged' temporality to the emergence of postcolonial projects, it has principally to do with the practical and theoretical failures of state-oriented nationalisms to continue the processes of decolonization. That failure was predicted by anti-colonial theorists like James Connolly and Frantz Fanon (with whose work postcolonial projects ultimately have more continuity than with Euro-American post-structuralism): it is an effect of what Fanon termed the 'sterile formalism' of bourgeois nationalisms.[8] Newly-independent state formations, constituted in accord with the political and cultural institutions of European modernity, arrested the processes of decolonization at the point which Marx would have designated mere 'political emancipation' and transformed the nation-state into the conduit for a newly-deployed international capitalism.[9] But it is precisely from this historical juncture that postcolonial projects gain the impetus to challenge the hegemony or self-evidence of the narratives of modernity that are borne in the post-independence persistence of what Ranajit Guha long ago termed 'the government of colonialist knowledge'.[10] For it is not simply a question of the extent to which nationalism replicates the political and institutional forms of the imperial state, enabling its continuity in the forms of a 'neo-colonialism', as has been noted by Reynaldo Ileto of the Philippines, or by Partha Chatterjee on India, or by many scholars working on Ireland.[11] It is, moreover, that the work of decolonization itself is interrupted in the occlusion of the multiple modes of resistance that emerged and continue to emerge on the interfaces of domination and insurgence.

For this reason, the modern state formation, not the moment of national independence in itself, is decisive for postcolonial projects. Rather than fetishizing the narrative that turns around the flagpole, postcolonialism, along with the 'subaltern' histories that have so often informed it, is devoted to the archaeology of practices and formations that are not subsumed in or determined by the nationalist project of the capture of the state. The 'post' in postcolonial refers not to the passing of colonialism but to the vantage point of critiques which are aimed at freeing up the processes of decolonization from the inhibiting effects of a nationalism invested in the state form. Such critiques make way for the reconstitution of alternative narratives which emerge in the history of our present, with its multiple contemporaneous rhythms and intersections.

Within postcolonial projects, then, a critique of state-oriented nationalisms and their modernizing institutions conjoins with the archaeology of non-nationalist or non-statist movements and formations which entail an entirely different temporal logic to that of the nationalist movement itself. The theoretical problem that arises here, as we have begun to see, is that these are movements that by and large have not been represented because, by definition, they cannot be within the developmental models of standard histories. Because they have not been absorbed into the logic of the state and its institutions, such formations have fallen outside the domain of history, just as they have never been adequately represented within the legal or statistical archives of the state. In postcolonial projects, accordingly, there constantly emerges a problem of representation that is inseparable from questions of the 'policing' of populations in the large sense that Foucault has elaborated.[12] It is to the question of historical representation that I now want to turn, taking up from the previous chapter the suggestiveness and the limits of two theorists, Walter Benjamin and Antonio Gramsci, who might be said to have been most influential on the historiographical dimension of postcolonial projects.

At this juncture, the collective engagement of postcolonial projects involves us in the work of what Benjamin termed, both against what then stood as orthodox Marxism and against liberal developmental 'historicism', a materialist historiography. Salient in his sketch of such a historiography in 'Theses on the Philosophy of History' is its pursuit of the modes of memory and transmission which traverse the apparently discontinuous but properly speaking occluded sites of marginalized social formations, sites that we might now designate 'subaltern'. Benjamin's emphasis falls on the staccato rhythms by which popular memory appears to irrupt, interrupting the forward movement of 'progress and development', in the form of the image which 'flashes up in a moment of danger'. Accordingly, the forms of popular memory seem irrevocably attached to discontinuity and recursiveness, the recursiveness to figures like Louis Blanqui, the proletarian leader of the 1848 revolution, whose name reverberates in the subsequent 'emergency' of the Paris commune. Such figures – and we might think of many within Irish popular memory – do not constitute a dialectic of progress, in which each previous stage of resistance or struggle is sublated progressively into the next. They constitute rather a negative dialectic which turns around the refusal of that forgetting which would be an acceptance of defeat and a relinquishment of the past to the determination of history. The apparent discontinuity of popular memory becomes the index of its refusal of developmental histories.[13] This discontinuity that Benjamin discerns in the forms of popular memory seems to echo with Gramsci's characterization of subaltern history in his 'Notes on Italian History'. But Gramsci, differently, designates the forms of subaltern narrative as 'episodic and fragmentary', implying their incompletion with regard to the longer project which is that of the capture of the state itself. Only at the moment when the counter-hegemonic forces of the subaltern classes succeed in capturing the state will their history be written in its full form. The prior discontinuity of their histories is less an issue of formal difference from dominant historiography than an effect of an insufficiently developed political consciousness. In this respect, we might understand Gramsci to be working primarily within a Hegelian Marxist model of the formation of a fully conscious proletarian subject.[14]

The conjunction implicit here between Benjamin's and Gramsci's projects is, then, also a disjunction or a displacement of each, one further marked by the peculiar dynamics of the colonial situation. The postcolonial tendency that I am seeking to adduce from a number of very different instances must negotiate with considerable tact an oscillating line between Benjamin's somewhat messianic celebration of the dialectical image and Gramsci's continuing insistence on the capture of the state as the end of counter-hegemonic work. That negotiation is determined by the circumstances and lessons of decolonization, in both its successes and its falterings. For it is in the first place questionable whether in fact the capture of the state and the consequent occupation of its institutions could serve the decolonizing project, where the very operation of the colonial state has been to erase, petrify or stigmatize as premodern the cultural and social institutions of the colonized. Although it is clear that virtually everywhere the emergence of the modern state form has involved at least the radical transformation and more often the elimination of cultural forms with a different or antagonistic logic, in the colonial sphere its generally violent imposition and survival has been marked simultaneously as the institution of strictly untraversable lines of difference. Virtually without exception the mode of differentiation has taken the form of racialization: cultural difference is marked as racial and racial difference is marked temporally as premodernity, as tradition.

In very different ways, Frantz Fanon and Benedict Anderson have written eloquently on the ways in which the effects of this racialization have given rise globally to nationalist resistance.[15] At the same time, the nationalisms that emerge from the racialized formation of the colonial state are burdened with a constitutive contradiction which continues to affect the post-independence state. For their emergence is tied to an effort at modernization that is intrinsic to the need to take over Western state institutions and to form a people constituted as modern political subjects. At the same time, however, the

appeal to distinct nationhood turns on the mobilization of selected or canon-
ized cultural forms which have been relegated by the colonial power, and in
turn by nationalism itself, to the frozen, extra-historical domain of 'tradition'.
The attempt to inhabit the institutions of the modern state and produce the
citizens that will function fully within them runs up against the problem that,
in order to do so, the state would have to write out the very traditions on
which national identity is predicated but which seem simultaneously to be
obstacles to modernization. It is in part this apparently aporetic predicament
that postcolonial projects seek to address by critiquing the terms in which
Third World nationalism and its Western critics have staged the dilemma. If
Gramsci valuably designates the terrain of the subaltern as a question for historical thinking, the colonial situation demands a redeployment of the ways
in which he ties that terrain to a state project.

Against the differently homogenizing logics of the colonial and the national
state, the force of Benjamin's materialism, famously 'brushing history against
the grain', is critical. In opposition to histories and projects so determinate in
their ends, the field of possibilities, of multiple temporalities and incommensurable ends that Benjamin's thinking suggests offers different openings both
historically and politically. My one hesitation over Benjamin's theoretical value
begins with a virtually formal concern but opens onto a rather different set of
questions that need to be framed within the postcolonial terrain. Benjamin's
emphasis falls on discontinuity and irruption, on what we might call the
occulting light of popular memory. Transposed into the spheres of colonial
states, such a representation of the forms of popular culture risks reproducing
that 'fetishization' of the popular of which Fanon everywhere speaks as a tendency of the partially assimilated but irredeemably racialized colonial subject,
a tendency which was no doubt his own at the moment of writing *Black Skin,
White Masks*. It is a tendency which goes hand in hand with the tendency to
regard popular culture as historically frozen, 'sclerotized', and which hyposta-
sizes discontinuity, fragmentation, and heteronomy as qualities of the colonized culture. Fetishization of the popular at once desires its fixity in a state of
'arrested development' that can only be unfrozen by the nationalist intellectual;
at the same time, it disavows the particularities of the cultural processes that
emerge in colonial conditions. Here, the real difficulty, which may perhaps
only be resolved initially by a certain wilful naiveté of approach, is to think at
once of the discontinuity and the transmission of cultural forms. We cannot
dispense with the acknowledgement of discontinuities without disavowing the
peculiar damage which colonialism everywhere inflicts on the cultural institutions of the colonized; at the same time, the question continually arises as to
how and in what forms – both genres and formations – the memory of resistance is transmitted to permit its remarkable recurrence across the long history
of colonialism and postcolonial states.

The kind of project I am implying here is not to be confused with the élite
nationalist historiography which renarrates the history of the nation as one in

which sporadic moments of popular resistance, sparked off by one or other colonial excess, give rise finally to a mature nationalist consciousness which was always already there in germ. In his essay 'Outlines of a Non-Linear Emplotment of Philippine History', Reynaldo Ileto begins by critiquing the élite nationalist replication of such narratives of modernity, signalled by their insistence on the processes of 'conscientization' as the means to politicizing the people. Over against that nationalist account of the processes of resistance and the formation of the 'people', Ileto approaches the figure of the bandits, leaders of indigenous insurrections thus stigmatized by Spanish colonialism, whose representation is principally spatial rather than temporal: they are marginal, external to the *barrio* and the *pueblo* which were the administrative nodes of Spanish rule, yet constantly impinging upon it.[16] As we have seen in the chapter 'Nationalisms against the State', Philippine anti-colonialism, from the Katipunan of the turn of the century through the Hukbalahap of the 1940s to the NPA of the present, has always involved a mutually inflecting intersection between élite nationalism and popular 'banditry'. Yet, from the perspective of the élite, the latter will always appear as discontinuous, emergent sporadically from the passivity of the people, awaiting conscientization in order to be politically effective. But while I would note here that the appearance of discontinuity is an ineluctable effect of the irrepresentability of certain processes within our standard modes of historiography – a constitutive blindness, if you like – my principal point is somewhat different. What Ileto crucially indicates is the extent to which the state formation, which emerges and transforms as an apparatus of counter-insurgency, is entirely imbricated in the very forms of popular culture which it discerns but cannot represent, except as the shadowy antagonist of the 'civility' it claims for itself. What appears in the statist narrative as premodern, atavistic and generally violent elements of colonial society are in fact reciprocally engaged in the emergence of the modern apparatus of the colonial state.

We can elaborate and clarify this point, in a way which will lead us to consider postcolonial hybridity in a different light, through an instance that I have written of elsewhere. The work of a number of historians has shown that Irish agrarian movements of the early nineteenth century were extraordinarily complex from a temporal perspective. Emerging as a response to the breakdown of eighteenth-century modes of political domination in Ireland, as well as to the continual transformations of agricultural production following the collapse of the Napoleonic wartime boom, these movements cannot be seen simply as reactionary or traditional: they represent continuously imaginative responses to new situations that participate in the production of modernity, but in ways which evidently cannot be seen as 'modernizing'. By the same token, they required on the part of the state a new response: the centralized national police force that functioned in Ireland long before any such 'modern' institution emerged in Britain. We can better understand this in terms of the forms or organization of the agrarian movements than in terms of any real force of intimidation they could deploy. Indeed, as Charles Townsend has pointed out, the British administration regarded these movements as constituting not anarchy but a kind of 'counter-legality' that was incommensurable with British notions of civil society and law but nonetheless had its own logic, however obscure or irrepresentable that might be.[17] Two factors are crucial here. One is the horizontal mode of transmission of rural unrest: agrarian disturbances communicated themselves with remarkable rapidity from locality to contiguous locality across large regions of Ireland without ever revealing any form of centralized or vertical leadership. The cultural forms which permitted this recurrent phenomenon remain somewhat obscure largely because they can only be retrieved from uncomprehending police documents and court records. This leads to the second point, which is the difficulty for history, as for the law, of apprehending any subject or agent in these disturbances: notions of agency which turn on the idea of an organizing figure are notoriously inadequate to deal with such social movements. In seeking ringleaders and outside agitators the state responded according to its own logic but remained entirely out of phase with the social forms through which popular resistance was articulated. In turn, the gradual organization of nationalist politics in nineteenth-century Ireland around individual figures and state-oriented institutions made it no less antagonistic than British administration to such movements.[18] Although nationalist historiography would see the emergence of a mass nationalist movement in Ireland as absorbing and refining prior popular modes, it would be possible to show that in fact bourgeois nationalism has constantly taken shape around its resistance to popular forms, from agrarian movements through Fenianism to post-independence republicanism.

These examples suggest that it is mistaken to understand subaltern formations as inhabiting a space outside the state and as unavailable to our representations because of that externality. We have to do, rather, with what happens and emerges at the interface between the state formation and subaltern formations, at that zone of interference between largely incommensurable social and cultural logics. Equally, these examples suggest the falsity of state-centred assumptions which, on the temporal as opposed to the spatial axis of representation, insist on the secondariness of the state to the prior and primordial violence of those it regulates. That is, it is the definitional myth of the state that it comes into being and claims its famous 'monopoly of violence' in order to impose its regularities, civility and laws on an unformed population whose very incommensurability to the state becomes the index of an innate violence. At the same time, the forms of the state conform to a reason which is effectively transhistorical, always the representative of the most modern, the most enlightened and civil forms of rule against which the colonized are measured and found backwards. The examples of Philippine banditry and Irish agrarian movements indicate, to the contrary, a double process: on the one hand, the interface between the state and the popular forms of the colonized produces a labile space in which each undergoes transformation; on the other, the very institutions which emerge in that space must relegate the recalcitrant forms for which they were instituted to anteriority, as signs of an incivility whose very persistence legitimates the violence of the state. In the discrepancy between the spatial and temporal logics of the colonial state, or the new nation-state, and the recalcitrant practices they must contain emerges a novel and unstable interface at which social formations are continually reconstituted. The differential dynamic that works constantly at that interface is peculiarly productive of contradictions. Into these contradictions postcolonial projects make their most effective interventions.

The historical texture of this zone, which extends from the cultural hybridity of translated forms to the productive antagonism of incommensurable social formations, is deeply marked by recurrent processes of displacement. This involves not so much an opposition between the continuity of the state form and the discontinuities of the popular, or indeed between popular traditions and modernization's disjunctions, as the continual transmission of memories both of resistance and containment into new institutional and quasi-institutional forms. Every moment of active antagonism between counter-hegemonic formations and the colonial state effects a displacement of each. In that displacement, new forms emerge which refunction elements of the old. In the case of the institutions of the state, this may be named adaptation or evolution; in the case of insurgent forms, the persistence of existent elements as vehicles for a new tenor is generally misrecognized as the persistence of residual forms while the moment of emergence is overlooked. In either case, this understanding of the processes involved 'at the interface' oblige us to rethink the concept of 'colonial hybridity'. Hybridity is only partially grasped as a process of cultural mixing and juxtaposition in which the traditional is combined and inflected with the modern or the native with the Western. Manifested in forms which range from artefacts like street ballads or tourist sculptures to institutions of state, what has been termed hybridity involves a continual and contradictory process of productive and reciprocal displacement of one another by cultural forms that are constituted as mutually incommensurable but are irreducibly contemporaneous with one another.

My final example of such processes brings these considerations to the contemporary moment. Northern Ireland, and in particular the cities Derry and Belfast, is the site of one of the most advanced, postmodern surveillance operations in the world. Computer databanks store information gained from listening devices trained on the panes of living-room windows or kerbside conversations; data from neighbourhoods, gathered both by such technologies and by the extensive and brutal house searches the British Army and the RUC. have conducted since the early seventies, is recorded on the same computers, so that at any checkpoint you may be asked not only your address but the name of your neighbour's dog; the normal daily routes of cars are recorded so that the slightest unusual movement of a given licence plate is registered and the vehicle tracked.[19] Clearly what is emerging here is a new mode of intervention and repression that has profoundly transformed the practices and institutions of the modern state formation. This transformation is an effect of the extensive militarization of a social conflict that emerged in a non-violent Civil Rights Movement in the 1960s and is enabled by the deployment of postmodern technologies. But it involves also a different logic of state intervention that constitutes a new continuum between state apparatuses that were directed at the non-violent or hegemonic regulation of private and civil society and the coercive force of the repressive apparatuses. It involves not only counter-insurgency strikes against paramilitary organizations, the criminalization of political activism and the corresponding expansion of the penal system, but more significantly the deep penetration of civil society by surveillance techniques through which the population is reconstituted as subjects of state authority rather than as citizens to be interpellated. That this new mode of state intervention, legitimated by the rhetoric of counter-insurgency that controls the media, emerges alongside continuing ideological appeals to consensus and the 'restoration' of democratic society in no way diminishes the novelty and probable irreversibility of what has emerged.[20]

Several studies have demonstrated how British counter-insurgency techniques used in Northern Ireland have gradually evolved out of numerous colonial campaigns, principally through the work of Brigadier Frank Kitson, whose *Low Intensity Operations* is regarded as the handbook for the containment of anti-colonial movements. Generally, such studies also regard Northern Ireland as a social laboratory for the emergent 'strong' or repressive state, envisaging the extension of practices developed there to the control of social movements in Britain, Europe and elsewhere in the industrialized world. This prediction accords with the established historical pattern of the transfer of modes of social control from colonies to the metropolis, but tends to obscure the specific conditions in Northern Ireland that have stimulated both the development of technologies of repression and the 'non-modern' forms of resistance with which they have been countered. Indeed, though the Northern Irish Troubles constitute probably the most massively documented conflict ever, remarkably little analytical or theoretical work has been done to comprehend its dynamics outside the conventional historical and journalistic terms that are often underwritten by the logic of counter-insurgency in any case. Most accounts, that is, replicate the narrative by which violence is seen as a sporadic and irrational expression of discontent which the state rationally seeks to contain from a position of externality and in the interests of benevolent reform.[21] Here, I want to go some small way towards suggesting how the implications of postcolonial work might inform a different kind of theoretical understanding of the Troubles and the conditions that have given rise to their particular dynamics.

Fundamental to the work of counter-insurgency, as Kitson makes quite evident, is the accumulation of in-depth intelligence not only about given militant organizations but about the communities which actively or passively sustain and shelter them.[22] The particular difficulty of this work in colonial situations lies not simply in the alienation of the potentially insurgent population from the colonial state, but in the cultural means and modes of communication that emerge, constituting intimate communities of knowledge and exchange that are deliberately opaque and external to the normative institutions of civil society. In Ireland, the culture of secrecy that has emerged in large part from the habits of a colonized population is a familiar and enduring phenomenon; in the racialized sectarianism of the Northern Irish state, the conditions for secrecy and the impenetrability of communities to the state have been intensified.[23] Such practices, clearly, are not survivals of premodern social formations but ones which have emerged in relation to modern colonialism. Indeed, to some extent, they may be most deeply embedded precisely where the advent of modernity has coincided with the effects of colonial segregation. Thus, for example, the development of Belfast through the nineteenth century was driven by the same forces as produced the English cities of the Industrial Revolution, with the result that its domestic and civic architecture and its urban planning to a great extent resemble those of northern England. But the religiously and ethnically segregated patterns of settlement and employment produced ghettoized urban spaces, especially to the west of the city where a displaced rural Catholic population gathered. In this respect, Belfast conforms remarkably to Fanon's characterization of the colonial city in *Wretched of the Earth*.[24] Modernity, rather than dissolving the effects of the colonial discriminations it considers atavistic or traditional, here in fact intensifies them. Accordingly, the forces of counter-insurgency in Northern Ireland meet with the peculiarly impenetrable forms of cultural intimacy that emerge where apparently modern geographies overlay colonial practices of domination. Consequently, we can understand the techniques of deep surveillance that have been brought into play as seeking to produce a simulacrum of what Raymond Williams described in the context of the modern 'realist novel' as the 'knowable community'; the postmodern authoritarian state finds itself simulating the intimate knowledges of the non-modern community.[25] It has also, in its turn, intensified the segregation of communities, particularly in urban spaces, through interventions which range from the construction of so-called 'Peace Walls' between Catholic and Protestant neighbourhoods to the extensive restructuring of Belfast for reasons of security and 'normalization'. The contemporary city is reconfigured around a relatively open yet deeply surveilled city centre, subject to urban renewal of a strikingly 'postmodern' and consumerist kind, and ringed by segmented working-class and sectarianized ghettos that are dominated by military and police barracks and surveillance towers.[26]

The least discussed issue in analyses of the emergence of new forms of repressive technique in Northern Ireland is the manner in which the intersection of non-modern, modern and postmodern practices and geographies produces the conditions for inhabiting, outwitting and resisting the systematically graduated violence of the state's incursions. Yet, within the context of the new repressive state, a series of tactics have emerged whose dynamics and conditions have not been extensively analysed. These would include the H-Block dirty protest and the hunger strikes of 1981, which emerged from the specific conditions of British criminalization policies directed at political prisoners, and which deployed the prisoners' bodies against the architecture and technologies of 'the most modern prison in Europe'.[27] But they would equally include the upsurge of cultural resistance over the last two decades, and especially the vital and entirely new genre of republican political murals. These murals mobilize in turn the architectural conditions of the nineteenth-century city, iconic traditions of post-Marvel comic books, and traditional republican iconography, in ways partly inspired by Latin-American examples.[28] The extraordinary productivity of cultural forms in the last thirty years of the Irish struggle is at once a matter of continuing anti-colonial struggle and, given the extent to which those evolving forms call in question the traditional modes of Irish nationalism, a critical instance of contemporary postcoloniality. Any understanding of such situations requires an exhaustive address to the materiality, the grain, of cultural conditions emergent on the interface between the state and quotidian cultural forms.

The analysis of contemporary cultural forms is matter for ongoing and collective projects within the context of Irish cultural studies. By way of conclusion, and in lieu of the more sustained project that is called for, I want to turn briefly to one of the most telling representations of the multiple temporalities of contemporary Belfast that we have, Ciaran Carson's *Belfast Confetti*.[29] This collection maps the complex, layered and shifting temporalities and geographies of Belfast through the intersecting optics of documentary history and anecdotal memories. Each optic is undercut, moreover, by the uncertainties produced, not only by the familiar vicissitudes of recall, but precisely by the recurrent incommensurabilities of documentary record and subjective recollection, a question constantly of the imperfectly totalizing framing of the event, the mapping of sedimented layers of memory and history:

> The left-hand frame of the photograph only allows us the 'nia' of Roumania Street, so I don't know what's going on there, but I'm trying to remember – was I there that night, on this street littered with half-bricks, broken glass, a battered saucepan and a bucket? In this fragment of a map, here is the lamp-post where I swung as a child, there is Smyth's corner shop; I can almost see myself in the half-gloom and the din.[30]

Historical documentation and personal recollection allegorize each other's indeterminacies, each opening gaps in the other's fabrications. These uncertainties are not merely posed ontologically but come into play through the heterogeneity of the cited cultural modes. Thus, throughout the volume, folk etymology and pun traverse and undermine the enterprise of philology that might fix the historical and linguistic origins of the city; official history, written out in archives and monographs, is out of kilter with the anecdotal procedures of popular memory; the forensic desire of the narrative poems encounters the elusive but suggestive uncertainties of intimate oral communication.

Many of the texts in the volume – which comprises poems, prose *récits* and interspersed haiku – explicitly inhabit the conditions of the postmodern repressive state as it cuts into the layered and dispersed temporalities of the city and its subjects. The prose text 'Intelligence' is among the most sustained of these, condensing Carson's fascination with military technology and tactics with the volume's recurrent motif of mapping and memory. (It may be recalled that the Ordnance Survey maps of Ireland were initiated and conducted from the early nineteenth century by the British military.) The text opens with the vista of night-time surveillance, apprehended not from the perspective of the operator but from that of the grounded denizen of the city:

> We are all being watched through peep-holes, one-way mirrors, security cameras, talked about on walkie-talkies, car 'phones, Pye Pocketfones; and as this helicopter chainsaws overhead, I pull back the curtains down here in the terraces to watch its pencil-beam of light flick through the card-index – *I see the moon and the moon sees me*, this 30,000,000 candlepower gimbal-mounted Nitesun by which the operator can observe undetected, with his infra-red goggles and an IR filter on the light-source.[31]

The reciprocation of watching ('Everyone is watching someone') then gives way to the imbrication of the hi-tech armament of the state with the often wittily uncanny lo-tech tactics of response. There doesn't even have to be a sniper for the whitewashed wall here to become an observing eye. Two very different modes of 'making visible' are at work in this passage as it slips between panoptical and situated viewing:

> Or we note in passing that some walls of the city have been whitewashed to the level of a man's head so that patrolling soldiers at night are silhouetted clearly for snipers; or that one of these patrolling soldiers carries a Self-loading Rifle with an image intensification night-sight; that paint bombs are usually reserved for throwing at the vision blocks of APCs and armored cars; and that passive observation is possible even on the darkest of nights, since the ambient light is amplified by this Telescope Starlight II LIEI 'Twiggy' Night Observation Device.[32]

The discrepancy between the eerie hyperreality of military hardware and the peculiar banality of the forms that resist it is intensified here by the aura of commodity fetishism registered in the relish for trademarks and acronyms. But the technological glitz remains susceptible to the interference of the location in which it is deployed, or incompatible hardware hampers the logic of its software:[33] 'the glitches and gremlins and bugs keep fouling-up, seething out from the hardware, the dense entangled circuitry of back streets, back-planes . . . '[34] Thus, unlike the squeaky newness of the military hardware, the 'barriers' that 'proliferated through the cities' are composed indifferently of the natural and artificial debris of modernity, withdrawn from the circuits of com-modity exchange to constitute a kind of 'memory-dump':

> bread-vans, milk-carts, telegraph poles, paving-stones, lime trees, chestnuts, hawthorns, buses, tyres, fishing lines, prams, JCBs, coal, shopping-trolleys, cement-mixers, lamp-posts, hoardings, people, sand, glass, breeze-blocks, cor-rugated iron, buckets, dustbins, municipal waste-bins, scaffolding, traffic sig-nals, garden sheds, hedges, milk-churns, gas cylinders, chimney-pots, snow, oil-drums, gates, crazy paving, orange crates, fences, weighing-machines, earth, automatic chewing-gum dispensers, news-stands, camera tripods, lad-ders, taxis, dismantled football stadia, bicycles.[35]

Virtually every item in this jumble of urban detritus is simultaneously an opaque repertoire of connotations, cultural and subjective. The literal barri-cades of Belfast streets, built to obstruct and delay the movement of the mil-itary, are simultaneously the 'random-riot' of memories and unruly associations, a defamiliarization of modern rationalities through a parody of the modernist and postmodernist device of the list that simultaneously deploys the dislocated temporalities of a (post)colonial culture.

There follows an extensive quotation from Bentham's *Panopticon*, which begins to read like a late Beckett text. The generalization of the metaphor of the panopticon ('Keeping people out or keeping people in, we are prisoners or officers in Bentham's *Panopticon*') perhaps derives as much from the politi-cal prisoners' inversion during the hunger strikes of their own imprisonment into an allegory of the repressive Northern state's relation to the nationalist population at large as it does from any Foucaultian apprehension of the ubiq-uitous extension of modes of discipline. Indeed, the implicit lesson of Ben-tham's text is that the very end of the disciplinary state, the isolation and therefore the control of its subjects, '*has been frustrated by occasional associa-tions*'.[36] Throughout Carson's text, these associations are at once implicitly social, referring to communities of resistance, and mnemonic. Indeed, the only 'blank zones' on the map of Belfast are the prisons, surrounded by the 'ubiquitous dense graffiti' of the city's sedimented architectures.[37]

The conclusion of 'Intelligence' with the unspoken story of the narrator's father not only inverts the trajectory of that classic and conclusive *Bildungsro-man* of modernity, Joyce's *Portrait of the Artist as a Young Man*, but in doing so also implies the simultaneity rather than the progressive seriality of multiple histories. As a volume, *Belfast Confetti* suggestively assembles the deep and sedimented histories of the city ('Belfast is built on *sleech* – alluvial or tidal muck – and is built *of* sleech, metamorphosed into brick'),[38] but does so not so much through a diachronic archaeology as through a synchronic section of their continuing play in the history of the present. We can understand it as furnishing a cultural map of postcolonial conditions, of the startling contemporaneity of incommensurable temporalities and narratives, narratives whose very recalcitrance to the disciplinary organization of truth and verisimilitude lies in their local specificity and various levels of impenetrability.

The challenge of postcolonial projects is precisely to seek to bring into constellation figures learnt from other locations with those that emerge in addressing the unrepeatable interfaces of the local and the global. What is learnt theoretically from the generalized, global condition of postcolonial formations signifies only in and through such address, an address which in turn radically transforms the nature of the theoretical questions that we continue to bring to bear.

TRUE STORIES
Cinema, History and Gender

Luke Gibbons has shrewdly remarked on the peculiar allegory of historical truth with which Robert Kee opens his celebrated documentary on Irish history, *The Green Flag*. First, an old Irishwoman appears, seated in her living-room, telling the tale of Ireland's centuries-long oppression by the British. Immediately after her tale, there follows a cut to a violent explosion. We then cut to Robert Kee himself, seated in a booklined study and equipped, unlike the old woman, with a large book. He proceeds to pose the questions on the nature of Irish history, on the reasons for the continuing violence, to which his documentary series will offer some answers. As Gibbons points out, this brief, imagistic series of narratemes implies a linkage between oral history, figured as a feminine and unreliable domain, and the violence it 'spawns', while suggesting a corresponding linkage between written history, civility and diagnostic explanation, figured – in a way that the prior image of the old woman throws into unwonted relief – as male.[1] In this chapter, I want to explore further the relation between civility and violence that is encoded in attempts to write the history of recent events in Ireland. In particular, I want to elaborate the connections between historical narrative and the articulation of the state and the domestic sphere as distinct but interlocked loci for civility, over against which 'incivility' is figured as violent and 'premodern' – and, under certain conditions, as 'feminine'. Later, I will turn to cinematic narratives which open onto a similar juncture of historical logic and gender constructions, domestic space, and the state. The films in question elaborate yet more tellingly the gendering of those spaces which is often left implicit in historical narrative.

I choose two recent historical works, not because they individually or together exhaust the field of histories of the Troubles, but because they will allow me to throw into relief two distinct models for historical explanation. The first is A. T. Q. Stewart's *The Narrow Ground*, less a history of the Troubles as such than an exploration of what its subtitle designates 'The Roots of Conflict in Ulster'.[2] The second is J. Bowyer Bell's *The Irish Troubles*,[3] probably the most thorough and certainly the lengthiest chronicle of the Troubles yet to appear. I use the term 'chronicle' advisedly: where Stewart's principal concern is with explanation via root causes, Bowyer Bell's overriding interest is in the chronological and serial documentation of the weekly events. The apparently contingent differences in length between the volumes are in fact an accurate register of the difference between a study designed to reduce events to recurrent causes and one whose structure of accumulation is strictly without possibility of conclusion.

In a most suggestive essay, 'The Prose of Counter-Insurgency', Ranajit Guha has distinguished two principal narrative modes for historiography, the paradigmatic and the syntagmatic. Deriving the terms from semiotics and linguistics via Roland Barthes' *Elements of Semiology*, Guha extends them to approach the historiographical framing of the 'event'. Taking as his object British accounts of Indian insurgency, he shows how these accounts, ranging from the first notification in panicked telegrams through forensic reports written after the fact to leisurely historical works, move from an initial representation of the event as a set of merely contiguous elements of insurgency and reaction to increasingly complex attempts at explanation governed by the need to compare and relate similar events within the Raj. This is what he designates as the shift from the syntagmatic to the paradigmatic axis of historical narrative, a shift of register from contingency to explanation.[4] Insofar as the levels of explanation shift from the pursuit of an immediate cause in the form of the 'outside agitator' to later investigations of the 'roots' of insurgency in those 'backward' social conditions which the modernity of British law is to eradicate, we might also want to argue that the emerging and increasingly general grammar of action involved here seeks to produce the level of the modern subject as at once observer and principle of history itself. That is to say, the function of narrative history is to be not merely explanatory with regard to immediate or contingent causes, but to grasp historical contingencies in relation to the larger narrative of history that is the emergence of the human properly speaking. In this case, the historian becomes the representative figure, eliciting order from the chaos of events in order to produce the form of history itself. The historian accordingly underwrites the project of the state that is to bring civility and modernity to the primitive and to maintain order in conformity with law.[5]

Within this organizing narrative, the state comes to contain the violence of events that never originates with it, to which it is always secondary. If order demands violence, that is because disorder and violence are the substrate of the state's civilizing process, a proposition which is the insufficiently stressed corollary of the Weberian maxim that the state has the monopoly of *legitimate* violence. Indeed, the very legitimacy of the state's use of force, as we have seen in the previous chapters, depends on the assumption that violence is at once prior to and antithetical to the state as principle. Accordingly, where the legitimacy of a given state and of its territory are in question, the representation of violence itself becomes a critical historiographical issue both with regard to the causes of violence (for there can be no representation of violence as event without simultaneously a causal logic) and with regard to the state's own use of force.[6]

In this respect, then, Northern Ireland is a peculiarly instructive domain, given that what is at issue is the legitimacy of states and their territories, the foundations of claims to legitimacy in actively contested historical narratives, and the mutual violence of the modern state and its antagonists. The perplexity of the historians is to account not simply for the intractability of the 'Irish Question' but for the recurrence of violence in the midst of a modern European state. One familiar mode of explanation relies predominantly on the ascription to the Irish of ethnic or cultural characteristics which are marked as premodern, usually in contradistinction to the modernity of British civil society and often in association with the continuing force of religious belief. This mode ranges of course from popular prejudice, instanced daily in the tabloid press, to academic historiography.[7] The explanatory paradigm of Stewart's *Narrow Ground* is a case in point to whose contradictions we will return. Another dominant mode, which we might see as the liberal to left version, seeks effective causes rather in the dynamics of the aberrant state form instituted by the Stormont Government in the fifty years of its existence and its social, political and economic consequences. This mode concentrates on the chains of action and reaction that constitute the events of the Troubles: Bowyer Bell's chronicle is exemplary of this approach, not least in the assumption implicit throughout that the resolution to conflict lies within reformist adjustments to the state itself.

Stewart's account asserts from the outset the persistence of certain *forms* of violence: 'Human nature does not change, except in the forms through which it is expressed. In Ireland, even the forms do not change.'[8] Indeed, one of the strengths of the work lies in its attention to the formal structures of violence and, in particular, to the dynamics of urban rioting.[9] This attention at least serves to open the question as to how violence emerges not simply as 'outbreak' but as an event – that is, as capable of representation at all. But Stewart's simultaneous commitment to the notion – based it must be remarked on the evidence of solely English sources – that 'Violence would appear to be endemic in Irish society . . . as far back as history is recorded' – [10] precludes any serious attention to the local and particularly historical specificity of the forms which violence has taken. The ways in which, in fact, the structures of riots, of agrarian disturbances or of rural guerrilla movements have modulated according to the forms of coercive strategy deployed against them by the state or by the transition from rural to urban industrial locations are never explored. Nor can his overarching paradigm address the specific means by which forms of resistance are both transmitted and refunctioned. Paradoxically, given Stewart's attention to the rhythms and forms of, for example, rioting in relation to the shifting demographics of urban space, the accumulated details reveal only the recurrence of the same forms. But his simultaneous disregard of the state as antagonist, rather than mere 'container', and of the question of resistance's transmission makes it clear that the historian's blindness is predicated very precisely on a perspective aligned with those whose function it is to 'contain violence'. The visual metaphor is suggested powerfully by the transhistorical 'pattern' he isolates:

> Much less attention has been paid to the regularity of the forms in which Irish violence is expressed . . . The primary pattern which emerges from the background of Irish violence is that of the secret army, the shadowy banditti 'on their keeping' in the mountains and bogs, whose lineage is traceable from the woodkerne of the sixteenth century to the provisional I.R.A. . . . Time and again, in describing the woodkerne, English observers remarked on the difficulty of coming to grips with them. After a raid on a planter's dwellings they simply melted away into the woods, or were metamorphosed into contented peasantry tilling the land or herding cattle.[11]

Striking in Stewart's assertion of transhistorical regularity is the evident contradiction between that assertion of formal continuity and the representation of discontinuity in the form of the 'fading' of the guerrilla. This historiography grasps as discontinuous and gapped the recurrence of social and cultural forms which cannot be fully represented within its perspectives. What escapes it is the logic of the subaltern insurgent's relation to a community to which s/he returns and whose reproduction occurs through narrative forms that are as incommensurable with the official historian's as the forms of community are to the state.[12] The identification between the forensic activity and vocation of the historian and the apparatuses of the state is correspondingly powerful.

But what distinguishes the historian's position from that of the functionary as such is his or her role as spectator rather than active participant in coercion. If the historian identifies with and legitimates the work of the state in the conjoined attempt to represent and contain the violence that constitutes the rationale of both, this happens precisely by virtue of the differentiation of the location of the historian from the state itself and his or her counter-identification with the domestic and civil spaces that the state's monopoly on force intends to protect. Like the cognate differential relation between culture and the state, this is more than a practical concern of the historian with the civil order and institutions that guarantee his or her professional practice: borrowing Arnold's formulation in *Culture and Anarchy*, we might remark that not only does 'history suggest the idea of the state', it suggests simultaneously the differentiation of social spheres within which the state relates to those domestic and civil spaces whose stability it guarantees.[13] Yet despite Stewart's insistence on the order that is requisite for the disinterested practice of scholarly history, what *The Narrow Ground* actually dwells on is the effective failure of the state to regulate its relations to civil and domestic society. For reasons embedded in its identification with the state's coercive project, the work cannot theorize what it nonetheless repeatedly and even fatalistically depicts: the state's failure to fully 'modernize' and incorporate the citizenry within an orderly civil society. For, ideally, history depicts the orderly regulation and differentiated emergence of the spaces of civil society that are in effect history's own condition of possibility. In Northern Ireland, as in other colonial sites, it is rather that an antagonism persists between social spaces that are structurally equivalent to, but by no means therefore identical with, the private or domestic and the state from whose vision they are occluded. Within such spaces, a different kind of narrative transmission proceeds, at odds with the ways in which the state seeks to form its subjects. The official coding for this transmission of recalcitrant matter is atavism, an atavism that significantly emerges in Stewart's haunted understanding as being remarkably at home in the domestic and civil institutions that look like those through which, normatively, the state would seek to interpellate and reproduce citizens. The following passage chimes suggestively with the allegorical opening of *The Green Flag*:

> So when we say that the Irish are too much influenced by the past, we really mean that they are too much influenced by Irish history, which is a different matter. That is the history that they learn at their mother's knee, in school, in books and plays, on radio and television, in songs and ballads. But they are influenced in another way by the past, as everyone is, and since they are often quite unconscious of this kind of influence, it is rarely discussed. It is the second kind of subjection to the past with which this book is chiefly concerned.
>
> At an early stage of the Ulster troubles, it became apparent that attitudes, words and actions which were familiar and recognizable to any student of Irish history, but which seemed hardly relevant to politics in the twentieth century, were coming back into fashion. This was not to be explained by the deliberate imitation of the past; it could be accounted for only by some more mysterious form of transmission from generation to generation. In many ways it was a frightening revelation, a nightmarish illustration of the folk-memory of Jungian psychology. Men and women who had grown to maturity in a Northern Ireland at peace now saw for the first time the monsters which inhabited the depths of the community's unconscious mind.[14]

We will pass over for the moment the peculiar contention that a state constitutionally founded as sectarian and regulated by a continual threat of violence could be said to be 'at peace'. Stewart's invocation of a 'mysterious form of transmission' as the cultural modality of popular memory and its effective demonization as some Jungian collective unconscious marks the all too typical lapse of historiography into the irrational fatalism that the limits of its peculiar modes of rationality impose. He falls back here on the recurrent obverse of the progressive ideology of modernity, an obverse required in order that the state project remain necessary: human nature never changes and civility is constantly arrested by atavism.

Before considering the different dynamics of Bowyer Bell's *Irish Troubles*, I want to address the conceptual occlusions that determine the many contradictions and limits of Stewart's work.[15] Among the more vexed questions in accounts of Irish history continues as we know to be that of Ireland's status: was it or not a colony, strictly speaking? Probably no work could better exemplify in its incoherences the consequences of denying – or, as in Stewart's case, ignoring – Ireland's colonial history than *The Narrow Ground*. It is not simply that much of the dynamics of Irish history, including but not limited to violence, can be understood far more comprehensively in relation to the experience of other colonial cultures. More importantly, the conundrum that lies at the heart of the work, the incommensurability between certain kinds of violence and cultural transmission, labelled atavistic, and the relatively early emergence of modern state institutions in Ireland, can scarcely even be articulated without Stewart's virtual mysticism unless the issue of colonial modernity be directly raised.

Let us shift the question onto a wider ground, one I shall return to in the next chapter. It is certainly no accident that in recent years the project of many of the Indian subaltern historians has shifted from their initial preoccupation with peasant and working-class insurgencies towards an interest in colonial modernity as it is expressed in the emergence of state institutions and the attempt by both imperial and nationalist thinkers alike to reform civil and domestic society.[16] What is at stake here, in distinction from Irish 'revisionist history' which deals with apparently similar issues, is not so much the success of such institutional interventions as their failures, unevennesses and margins of excess. The question which arises concerns what happens at the point of contact between radically incommensurable cultural formations where one seeks by force to impose itself on the other. What kinds of cultural formations emerge from the encounter between differing degrees of recalcitrance and coercion? To what extent can these emergent formations be understood within the terms of tradition and modernity, where both are modified in the encounter? What kinds of subjectivities emerge along the multiple zones of interface that range from subaltern locations, subject primarily to direct domination with little cultural interpellation, to élite nationalist formations which, by virtue of extensive cultural assimilation, replicate imperial forms but are never quite the same? How do we understand the effects of such encounters and the articulation of such subjectivities at levels from the most intimate aspects of daily bodily practices (hygiene, conversation, the expression of affect, the assumption of gender) to the larger symbolic forms by which cultural identities are articulated (cultural forms and tastes, language use, political institutions, etc.)? What is the continuum of violence involved, where the very passive resistance to, for example, the imposition of alien forms of hygiene or labour may be construed from the colonizer's perspective as the symptom of an uncivilized resistance to modernity and as, accordingly, the symptom of an inherently violent premodernity? What is the role of such recalcitrance or resistance in actually constituting new forms of state, as opposed to being merely the object of coercion by an already constituted and more advanced form of state? What, in sum, is emergent in the colonial situation at the unstable interface between modernity and non-modernity?

What happens, then, in the face of events which deny the generic canons of historical or even aesthetic verisimilitude? What occurs in the face of conjunctures which seem to scramble the distinction between paradigmatic and syntagmatic axes that order the moments through which happenings are narrated as historical and historicizable events? The force field of violence which emerges on the interface between the modern or postmodern state and non-modern social formations, an interface characteristic of colonial situations, is precisely one in which the narratability of the event enters into crisis. This is at once a matter of social contestations over narrative modes and, more importantly, an effect of the multiple series of trajectories that may be thrown up from the interference of incommensurable social logics. Events and their narrations fissure into an unpredictable set of provisional and performative possibilities that can be reduced neither to the stability of paradigmatic forms nor to the mechanical syntagma of causes and effects.

If Stewart's *Narrow Ground* is avowedly paradigmatic in intent, it would not be difficult to read Bowyer Bell's *The Irish Troubles* as not only its syntagmatic antithesis, but as, moreover, a latter-day naturalist text. Parts of the prologue, indeed, read like extracts from Liam O'Flaherty's *The Informer* and are clearly enamoured of film noir atmospherics.[17] But apart from these stylistic affectations and the penchant for metonymic detail (Bernadette Devlin, for example, is virtually inseparable from her miniskirt at every appearance), what is most salient in the text is its elaboration of events as a cumulative series of causes and effects: history appears as a virtually mechanical set of actions and reactions that operate largely within entirely pragmatic horizons of calculation and response. In this respect, Bowyer Bell's work is far more able to grasp the Troubles as an effect of interactions between the state and antagonistic social groups than is Stewart's, and far more able to engage with the contemporary logic of events rather than seeking explanations in the return of atavism.

A striking exception to this is his treatment of the hunger strikes, which we can regard as symptomatic of the limit point for such writing. Space does not allow for an adequate treatment of the republican campaign against the criminalization of political prisoners to which the 'dirty protest' and the hunger strikes from 1976 to 1981 were central: this is matter for a further project. What I would want to assert at this point is that these actions need to be understood as events that occur on the interface between non-modern cultural formations and a modern, indeed, largely postmodern, penal apparatus. The immediate site of that interface is the body of the prisoner and the cell, but only insofar as those are not seen as delimited and given but as themselves already profoundly structured by state and culture. Nor should this be misunderstood to suggest that there is a simple opposition between a non-modern culture of the prisoners and the mixed modern and postmodern culture of the penal apparatus: on the contrary, it is precisely the instability and multiplicity of possible relations and the tactical deployment of that instability which informs the protests at every moment.[18]

Containment of the cultural significance of the hunger strikes in the liberal and conservative media in both Ireland and Britain, ranging from popular to academic accounts, has tended to proceed by invocation of the atavistic or religious nature of the rhetoric and imagery that accrued to them. These phenomena are assumed to be the projections of the prisoners' own psychic formations and symptoms of the premodernity of republican ideology. Once again the intervention of the state and its apparatuses is seen as secondary to the irrational and potentially violent forces of premodernity; its productive role in the constitution of coercive institutions and the logic of resistance to them is correspondingly underplayed. The subterranean powers of myth are seen to defy the rationality of the state and the corollary to that danger is that, if not contained by the state, such forces will overwhelm civil society itself, imposing an irrational will on the supposedly non-coercive order of existing society. Republican resistance comes rapidly to bear the markers of fascism, a simplification that subserves the extraordinary coercive powers of the state.

What I would argue, picking up a point already made in the chapter 'Nationalisms against the State', is that the historiographical project and the narratives of liberal civil society which it underwrites need to produce myth at the very point at which the incommensurability of civil society and alternative social formations becomes contradiction. Mythopoeia, projected onto others, serves to rationalize the very excesses of state power that effectively call in question its claims to legitimacy. Indeed, one of the paradoxes of the Weberian definition of the state is that its claim to monopoly of the use of force depends on the virtuality of its violence: from the moment that state power becomes visible and regular in its exercise against its subjects, the legitimacy it derived from the appearance of consensus is evidently in question. Such is precisely the point of manifestations like prison protest and hunger striking, which obey a quite pragmatic logic within the very terms the modern state apparatus establishes. But unlike guerrilla warfare as such, which openly questions the state's monopoly of violence, modes of *apparently* passive resistance stage their antagonism to the state by performing the excess of *its* violence as a means to questioning its legitimacy. And unlike guerrilla warfare, which can be grasped and attacked as an illegitimate *agency* operating with determinate ends, 'passive resistance' stages subjection as the condition of subjecthood and accordingly seems to exceed in its performance, rather than in its achievements, any of the ends for which it ostensibly aims.

Bowyer Bell grasps the perplexity which the prison protests produced in staging the incommensurability between what he regards as British and Irish 'games'. But he is finally unable to understand that incommensurability except as one between atavism and pragmatism:

> What the strikers sought was certain if they remained steadfast. And so, like the opponents, they did. And so each won what had been sought and each was rewarded in kind – the British with the trappings of a conventional triumph in what had been a spiritual war and the Irish with the triumph of a spirit willing

to suffer all. This Irish republican victory was perceived as such not simply by the wretched and angry of the Third World or the Catholic Irish attracted by the atavistic traditions of old but by many who perceived the confrontation as one of will against power. The British may have taken the marbles but that was another game. The Irish game was different and none could count the returns though all could count the cost.

If the will lasted to the final breath, this spiritual victory could not be denied: the game was in the playing not the winning. The ten died and so suffering won. They had their lives taken for their friends and for the ideal, the dream. This the pragmatic, confident, and conventional missed, especially the British, as they had always missed the values of an island so different from their own.[19]

In the context of so polarized an understanding of national characteristics, it seems necessary that Bobby Sands, the first of the hunger strikers to die, be represented not only as martyr and symbol within an Irish Catholic 'atavistic tradition' but as representative of the sacrificial insurgent in general:

All struggles offer stereotypes and symbols; most of all they offer an opportunity for the young absolute in their commitment, emboldened by their own dedication, to sacrifice . . . And so it was for the Cypriot Greeks of EOKA or the Jews of the Irgun and so it is for the Palestinians or the Muslim Brothers or the Basques. Each acolyte arrives in a different context with a different historical and ideological baggage, shaped by special cultural forces and personal predilections, but all come absolutely dedicated to their faith and to the chance to sacrifice to redeem the ideal. Sands was simply the typical pared down to the intense and burning core.[20]

It is, of course, Bowyer Bell who is here mobilizing the stereotype of the fanatic terrorist as a substitute for explanation, as Stewart does the Jungian unconscious as a substitute for the analysis of cultural transmissions. The stereotype as fetish, to borrow from Homi Bhabha's phrasing,[21] functions here as a kind of hystericized symbol, a particular that becomes representative of a universal in order to cover the kind of fissuring that the event of the hunger strike causes for historical narrative. It is no accident that Bowyer Bell's own narrative mode shifts from his standard account of the ongoing pragmatics of antagonistic actions and reactions onto the axis of symbolic paradigms: his own perplexity doubles that of his 'pragmatic' and 'conventional' British, producing the polarization between Irish fanaticism and reason of state within which the dynamics of the event itself become frozen and ultimately illegible.

The structuring polarity 'fanaticism/reason' that occupies the temporal axis, posing fanaticism as an atavistic antagonist to civil society, and in particular to modern modes of 'governmentality',[22] is supplemented over and again in *The Irish Troubles* by another polarization on the spatial axis. That is the one that persists between both the state and the insurgent on the one hand, and ordinary domestic life on the other:

> The poor uninterested in politics, the vast majority, did not march or protest, throw stones, contribute to the UVF, or buy *Republican News*. They never wanted more than peace and quiet and a job, perhaps a wee house and money for the pub, a new coat, a turkey at Christmas. They had narrow, everyday lives, dreaded that their children would volunteer for a dirty war, lived in quiet desperation or emigrated to other miserable prospects but without the army on the street . . . They filled the small houses, enjoyed their children and the telly, had a dog, went to the pub, had a flutter on the pools, had small hopes, short views. They coped . . . A focus on the small, the one lane, the old parish almost always indicated everyone coping.[23]

Bowyer Bell's patronizing tone is of course the historian's equivalent to criminalization, disjoining the populace from any organic relation to the 'terrorist', and the alibi for the culture of the expert who protects the uninterested citizenry from forces they can neither control nor understand. Here, naturalist backdrop becomes the rationale for the postmodern state, in the sense of the state as a hi-tech remote control apparatus which operates in the absence of the participatory public sphere that was the imaginary space of modernity.[24]

At the horizons of this polarity, however, a considerable degree of instability insists. For what is opposed to what? On the one hand, the domestic space of quiet but desperate ordinary life is opposed to the symbiotic violence of the state and its insurgents 'out there'; on the other, domestic life and the state that guarantees its security are opposed to the atavistic forces of terrorism that threaten both. But then again, the case of the hunger strikes, where those ordinary streets produce and sustain martyrs and heroes, suggests that domestic life and its reproduction of the narratives that legitimate insurgency in fact oppose the state. We are back in the domain of Robert Kee's *The Green Flag* or of Stewart's popular Irish histories, and no less at the heart of what the state fears.

The problematic nature of this instability can best be highlighted by recalling how important the capture of the domestic space has been to the rhetoric and practice of counter-insurgency. I intend 'capture' in both a literal and a metaphoric sense. On the one hand, the literal surveillance and invasion of the domestic spaces of Republican activists – their homes, safe houses, clubs and streets – has contributed to sustaining and intensifying the IRA's campaign. On the other, the criminalization policy which was the second wave of counter-insurgency strategy, after the indiscriminate internment of suspected activists and the isolation of rebublican districts, depended crucially on the separation of 'terrorists' from their communities both literally, by imprisonment, and metaphorically, by the deployment of a dehumanizing rhetoric. Central to the rhetoric is the construction of the terrorist as fanatical, pathological, hypermasculine, and incapable of affect. This involves often enough the contradictory representation of the activist as at once affectless and atavistically driven by emotion. The intent here is less to isolate the activist from any possibility of relation to community, though that hope has never been abandoned. The purpose is rather to legitimate the state's counter-insurgency project by denying that the guerrilla struggle might have an organic relation to those communities from which it derives an entirely different order of historical legitimation and support. What emerges is a set of entwined but often contradictory narratives: at one moment, atavism is the pathological aberration of a handful of 'men of violence' which upsets the normative relation between domestic life, civil society and the state; at others, atavism is the property of whole communities who are accordingly 'not yet' capable of full participation in civil society. What cannot be admitted is the possibility of communities whose formation, domestic and civil, is for historical reasons external and antagonistic to the state itself, and particularly the existence of communities whose experience of subjection to the modern state provides the dynamic for social imaginaries that cannot be contained easily within the narratives of modernity.

The problem, then, is twofold: on the one hand, to fragment the canons of verisimilitude which stabilize the various elements that constitute the ideological 'self-evidence' of the modern state formation; on the other, the longer and more arduous project of inventing other modes of narrative, of historicization, of representation, which might counter the extraordinary weight of self-evident truths without stabilizing or fetishizing alternative formations into fixed oppositional locations. I have argued in the previous chapter that this will involve learning from 'postcolonial projects' and a new understanding of the formations of culture. What I shall analyse in the following section, in relation to more widely disseminated cinematic narrative, is the crucial function of the construction of gender positions in both official and counternarratives. These cinematic representations, we will see, tend to pin down the normative and delimit aberrational forms of subjectivity to stabilize the ground for social relations in general.

II

In what is possibly the most canonical of all the founding texts of aesthetics, Aristotle presents what is at once a law for verisimilitude and a division of disciplinary or generic domains. What distinguishes poetry from history, he argues in the *Poetics*, is that, whereas the latter narrates all that has proven to be possible, poetry (or drama) must narrate only that which seems probable. It is, of course, a classical moment of foundation, insofar as what 'seems probable', that which has the striking self-evidence of 'seeming true', must seem so because it conforms to the *doxa* which it simultaneously produces. Aesthetic truth, in fact, bears little relation to what is true or even to what is probable, since its seeming true is an effect of its relation to convention rather than denotation.[25] In this respect, *Oedipus Rex* is typical; the powerful effect of truth which the tragedy exerts derives not from the empirical probability of a man's killing his father *and* marrying his mother but from the scandal such a *possibility* self-evidently evokes in the play's audiences. The power of the affect which the transgressions produce confirms the legitimacy, the self-evidence, of the laws which have been transgressed. And, secondly, it is the narrative organization of a series of 'improbabilities' (Oedipus' abandonment and survival, his discovery of his origins, his encounter with his father, his saving of Thebes, his marriage to his mother, the plague that 'results') towards the combined ends of *anagnorisis* and *peripeteia*, rather than the intrinsic likelihood of any given event or narrative element, which produces the effect of probability.

At the risk of seeming to perform a too abrupt and improbable shift of register, let me turn to another dramatic work for which *peripeteia* and *anagnorisis* in the domain of sexuality and politics are crucial; namely, Neil Jordan's *The Crying Game*.[26] I shall assume knowledge of the narrative of the film and, rather than engage in playing the game of the surprise that dare not speak its name, list instead a string of 'improbabilities' around which the narrative is structured in order that we may proceed to decipher the organization of the narrative elements by which what is, in the naive sense, historically unlikely accrues the force of self-evidence.

In the relatively long history of the current Irish Troubles (1969–95), the IRA has not resorted to taking hostages, an act which precipitates the narrative of *The Crying Game*. Such an act would infringe the forms of mobility through which it has been possible for the longest ever urban guerrilla war to have been conducted in the face of around thirty thousand troops and paramilitary police. Furthermore, tactics aside, it may be that hostage-taking transgresses the symbolic logic of the contemporary struggle, as Allen Feldman's recent ethnographic work on Northern Ireland would suggest.[27] But supposing a hostage were to be taken, the likelihood of the IRA's choosing to kidnap a *black* British soldier is infinitesimal. As Jody himself intimates, the presence of black people is sufficiently uncommon in Ireland that nothing would be more likely to attract attention at a small rural fairground than an Irish lass in the company of an Afro-Caribbean man. Indeed, the policy of confining off-duty British soldiers to barracks in Northern Ireland bespeaks the fact that it is enough to be a soldier to stand out. That said, however, it is no less unlikely that, as Jody claims, Ireland is 'the only place in the world where they call you nigger to your face': anyone who is aware of the intensity of institutional and informal racism in contemporary Britain will be surprised at such a claim from a Caribbean who has grown up in Tottenham.

As the narrative proceeds, Fergus Hennessy becomes increasingly infatuated with Jody, is reprimanded for fraternizing with the prisoner, yet is permitted to spend the last night with him and to conduct the execution alone. It is perhaps enough to remark that an underground organization with the longevity and effectiveness of the PIRA has not survived through such breaches of military discipline or logic.[28] As Jody attempts to escape, British troops in Saracens and helicopters launch an exceptionally violent assault on the PIRA's rural 'safe house'. Though it is possible to read this scene as both an acknowledgement of British military brutality in Ireland and an indication of the discrepancy between the PIRA's lo-tech insurgency and the might of state violence, it is nonetheless one more improbability: Northern Ireland, as we have seen, has been the exemplum and the experimental theatre of what Brigadier Frank Kitson designated and theorized as *Low Intensity Operations*. Of all things, the British army has been at pains to avoid the possibility of scandalizing domestic public opinion by conducting such high-powered raids and thereby highlighting the violence of the state. Furthermore, the intent of low intensity operations is to de-emphasize the military conflict in the occupied zones in order to permit the undermining of solidarity between guerrillas and community – a point to which we will return shortly.

Some further improbabilities: Fergus arrives in London incognito and finds work on a building site where he is seen throughout the film working alone. Though the racial slurs directed at him are within the experience of any Irish person working in Britain, the probability of his finding work in the building trade without the company of other 'Paddies' is minimal. Less improbable, perhaps, and one of the director's few overt manipulations of point of view, Fergus entirely fails to observe the transvestite clientele in the Metro, a clientele which only becomes evident on screen after his discovery of Dil's sex and which, the subtext of the film is at pains to emphasize, would have been unfamiliar to him in his Northern Irish 'local', the Rock. (The names of Fergus's and Jody's respective hangouts are heavily allegorical within the larger symbolic structure of the narrative.) As we shall see, these apparently disconnected observations both bear in fact on Dil and Fergus's relation to communities.

Let me complete this enumeration for now – it could doubtless be extended from others' perspectives – by commenting on the improbability of Peter's resort to an evidently suicidal attack on the old judge and his bodyguards when Fergus, neatly bound by Dil, fails to appear. Though the PIRA has lost many volunteers in the course of its operations, it has not been characteristic of *any* Northern Irish paramilitary group to engage in suicidal operations. His death, of course, has some specific dramatic functions: it underscores the certain fate from which Dil has saved Fergus; it furnishes Jude's otherwise uncharacteristically rash and headlong pursuit of Fergus with an emotional rationale; it permits the one-on-one confrontation between Fergus's 'two women' which is the film's significant denouement. But its dramatic function is ideologically overdetermined in a way which will allow us to elaborate the surpluses of signification which organize and trouble the film's economy. For Peter is a 'typical terrorist', at once emotionless ('I'm getting emotional. And I don't want to get fucking emotional – you understand, Hennessy?') and fanatical, and in consequence both ruthless and self-destructive. The pathology of what is called terrorism is held to derive from an emotional repression sublimated in violence; its 'pathologic' is intrinsically contrary to

humane and often confused values such as those which inflect Fergus's relation to Dil.[29] It is possible, given the contemporary context of 'terror network'
media imagery, to further associate Peter's suicidal attack with popular psy-
cho-racial representations of Islamic terrorists that collapse into portraits of
terrorism in general with the same regularity as Beirut is conflated with
Belfast. But that connection is in fact already prepared for by a more embedded conflation of the virtually coeval stereotypes of the terrorist and the Irishman, a conflation whose popular circulation probably originates with the
Fenian campaigns of the 1860s. In this conflation, the Irishman is drawn to
terrorism because of the violent and sentimental or fanatic nature of his racial
psychology.[30] Violence becomes a racially rather than socially or historically
conditioned characteristic. Indeed, we can see that the pathology of the *individual* terrorist is a repetition of the atavism of the community that concerns
the historian. Jody has alluded to this popular understanding of the Irish conflict and of PIRA 'terrorism' earlier when he remarks to Fergus 'You people
never give up, do you?' and contrasts their vocation with his 'job'. What is
underscored here, and recapitulated in the symbolic difference between cleav-
ing to the Rock and going down the Metro, is a distinction between Fergus's
fundamentally atavistic and obsessional sense of self and one characterized by
modern or postmodern forms of alienated labour which, less paradoxically
than may at first seem, correspond to Jody's humanity. In effect, accession to
full humanity is defined by one's not being identified with a particular job:
only slaves and fanatics are defined by and bound to their work as to an identity; alienated labour, on the contrary, is the very condition of individuation.

As others before have pointed out, such an essentializing portrait of the
'terrorist' requires that the figure be produced through a rigorous separation of
the political militant from any dynamic relation to a community, a culture or a
history.[31] As John Hill has put it, in a comment whose relevance to other insurgent communities is not difficult to see, 'It is only metaphysics or race, not history and politics, which offer an explanation of Irish violence'.[32] As Jordan has
been only too keen to point out, in general his films seek precisely to treat of
Irish violence in metaphysical terms.[33] But the distinction between a racial and
a metaphysical explanation is hard to sustain once it is recognized that a metaphysics which speaks in the name of an essential human subject underwrites
the racializing process which speaks to the 'in-adequacy' of certain groups or
cultures in relation to the end embodied in the human archetype. In this
respect, Frantz Fanon's succinct comment on black/white relations within a
universal schema in *Black Skin, White Masks* is no less, if differently, applicable
to the Irish: 'The black is not a man . . . The black man wants to be white. The
white man slaves to reach a human level.'[34] Ironically, then, it is the black
Jody's parable of the scorpion and the frog, reiterated by Fergus to Dil at the
end of the film, that states it most simply: 'It's in [their] nature.'

In these respects, *The Crying Game* recapitulates a set of ideologemes
which structures popular representations of what is named terrorism and

intersects with another set of racial stereotypes concerning the Irish. It conforms, that is, to the *doxa* developed simultaneously in historical works and whose self-evidence it repeats and extends. Its effect of verisimilitude derives from the organization of its improbabilities around certain ideological givens: that terrorists and the Irish are *by nature* fanatical, pathological, atavistic and, by virtue of these characteristics, lack full humanity. Requisite to such representations is their radical severance of insurgency from any historical ground which might give it a rationale beyond Fergus's wretchedly banal 'I think you should get out of my country'. Insurgency is severed from any articulate, however contestable, programme for social transformation, and, above all, from any relation to the subordinated communities without whose at least passive acquiescence and often active support a long-lasting guerrilla campaign is unthinkable. In this, of course, the film corresponds to the strategies of the British and Irish states in those military and censorship policies that have attempted to cut off the insurgents from any base in the community, to transform political violence into 'mere' crime by the policy of criminalization, to restrict Sinn Féin and the IRA's capacity to articulate their rationales and policies by strict media censorship, and thereby to depict the armed struggle as the 'irrational' and 'mindless' malevolence of 'men of violence', a phrase which will gather resonance for us as we proceed.

The sets of improbabilities that I have identified in *The Crying Game* and related to popular ideologemes more generally are reinforced by cinematic conventions whose regularities constitute an effective discourse.[35] At the core of the genre is the narrative motif of the good-hearted man who is drawn into political insurgency by generally humane motives, is at some point repelled by his own or others' violence, seeks to leave the organization but is prevented from doing so by the fanaticism of his erstwhile colleagues. Both Fergus's story and his name allude clearly to these generic conventions (*Hennessy* is the title of Don Sharp's 1975 film as well as Fergus's surname.) Throughout, political violence is decontextualized and attributed principally to pathological individuals; by extension, Ireland stands as a figure for metaphysical rather than socio-political predicaments, as a figure, that is, for a violent and chaotic enigma which defies rationality. As already suggested, this figuration of Ireland relies on historically embedded stereotypes of Irish irrationality and on a sustained 'contrast between characteristics of Irish society and those of an apparently advanced and modern civilization'.[36] Hill identifies several further regularities whose relevance to *The Crying Game* will merit elaboration. Firstly, the counter to the investment in political violence is the good woman who seeks to redeem the terrorist, a motif extended into the 'contrast between a commitment to violent activity . . . and conventional family life'.[37] Secondly, in keeping with such films' adherence to Anglo-American realist modes, individual psychology becomes the privileged mode of explanation, whether of the terrorist pathology or of the good man's need to get out. This emphasis on individuation corresponds evidently to the abstraction of the individuals and their acts from any relation to specific communal experiences, giving way, in a paradox intrinsic to individualism, to an entirely decontextualized universality. As Hill puts it, 'The individualizing logic of both narrative and realism necessarily favours the private and personal at the expense of the public and political.'[38] These characteristics have, thirdly, a logical correlative: implicit endorsement of 'violence at the hands of the state', since 'the reliance on the police for narrative resolution must inevitably obscure that it is the legitimacy of the state which is itself a political question'.[39]

Hill's essay indicates the extent to which patterns of ideological self-evidence intersect constantly with the longer duration of generic verisimilitude. By and large, The Crying Game itself rehearses that intersection to the extent of its conformity to genre. Hence, Fergus's individuation of himself when he goes into hiding in London underwrites the individuality that already sets him apart from his fellows in the IRA and confirms the film's larger but unstated erasure of any communities, whether the army, the Catholic 'ghetto', or the émigré community in London. What Jody calls Fergus's 'nature' is opposed to the pathology of terrorism and disposes him to the kindness around which the narrative turns and which makes of him, in the language of identificatory narratives, a 'sympathetic' character. As will already be apparent, however, it is considerably more difficult to follow Hill's other generic elements – domesticity and the sanction of state violence – through The Crying Game. The relationship between Dil and Fergus seems at most a parody of 'normal' domestic love while in the resolution of the narrative the intervention of the state seems unusually remote: unlike their function in other such films, the police enter only as a kind of afterthought in The Crying Game. The genre seems alluded to but displaced. What I want to explore here is how the exceptional generic self-consciousness of The Crying Game, in keeping with its mobilization of the figure of drag and, indeed, of performance at every level, at once displaces and reinscribes the borders of ideological and generic modes of representation, but does so in ways that produce an excess of possible signification that the film can neither control nor elaborate.

In the first instance, Fergus's story seems to rehearse all the generic conventions identified by Hill: the good-hearted terrorist whose nature allows him to identify with the hostage and to engage in a loving and protective relationship with a woman which, in this case quite literally, constitutes a tie to hold him back from further violence. Only the discovery that Dil is not what she seems interrupts this narrative. This interruption floods the preceding scenes with an ambiguity which, though invested in sexuality, opens onto the larger questions of verisimilitude with which the film in its generic self-consciousness continually plays: what was Jody's intent in sending Fergus to Dil? Has he read Fergus's 'latent' homosexual desire? If Dil's sex and her gender are at odds, what does it mean to have a 'nature'? What does it mean for Jody to say 'women are trouble' or for Fergus to remark, on seeing Dil's photograph, 'She'd be anyone's type'?

This last assertion, in effect 'fatal' for Fergus, potentially opens a whole series of questions as to type, genre and classification; that is, to the self-evidence of categories. The recurrent metaphysical dilemma as to the relation between semblance and truth, which Jordan derives most immediately from Hitchcock,[40] turns on this visual misrecognition and is accordingly concentrated on the domain of sexuality, evoking the incommensurability of sex and gender. Fergus's 'she'd be anyone's type' is met later by the sphinx-like barman Col's aborted warning to Fergus: 'Something I should tell you . . . She's on.' This displacement of the promise of truth (Fergus: 'She's what?') by Dil's lip-synched rendering of 'The Crying Game' shifts the register of gender identity from the visual evidence of biological sex, what Freud calls 'the anatomical sex distinction', to that of performance.[41] After the fact, it becomes evident that Fergus's relation to Dil has always already been a performance, artfully directed by Dil, at times with the assistance of Col:

> (In the Indian restaurant)
> Dil: Now's the time you're meant to do something, isn't it?
> Fergus: Like what?
> Dil: Make a pass or something? Isn't that the way it goes?
> Fergus: Must be.

It is also, as Dil's performance of the song stylizes, the mimesis or citation of roles:

> (In the Metro)
> Dil: So what do you want with me, Jimmy?
> Fergus: Want to look after you.
> Dil: What does that mean?
> Fergus: Something I heard someone say once.[42]

Through this emphasis on the performative constitution of gender, *The Crying Game* distantiates itself from the ethic of realism, which insists on bringing individual desires into conformity with what is given as the facts of life. The universality claimed by canonical realism derives from the naturalization of 'second nature', in Lukács' term, by the repetition of the narrative of the individual's coming to see, and come into relation to, the transhistorical truth of convention; that is, 'human nature'.[43] The parodic relation of *The Crying Game* to realistic genre, and specifically to the IRA thrillers analysed by Hill, lies in Fergus's coming to cite his masculinity as he wittingly and repeatedly performs his role as Dil's lover. Part of the success of the film lies equally in the difficulty an audience has in not seeing Dil as a woman, even after his sex has been revealed or her hair has been shorn: both performances are predicated on a witting disavowal of the already seen. And, in this sense, the film equally inverts Freud's version of the Oedipus story, a version utterly informed by the ethic of realism insofar as the male child's polymorphous desires are finally constrained to submit to the visual evidence of what seems to be the case. A closer reading of Freud, however, shows that what has the force of fact can only gain its reality-effect from a prior fixation of the infantile psyche on the genital zone that is part of the infant's 'normal' development.[44] For what Fergus disavows is not what Dil lacks but what Dil has, and accordingly his assumption of a male gender is predicated on the dissociation of fact and performance, truth and verisimilitude.

At no point, however, is desire allowed priority over the self-evidence of performance. Paradoxically, the performance of gender for Dil and Fergus is stabilized by the proscription of the enactment of desire through the performance. The undecidedness of Fergus's affect in relation to Dil is in fact crucial to his maintaining a heterosexual male identity: we may ask what the 'nature' of his desire for Dil is, whether he 'likes her better as a man' when he cuts her hair, whether he 'really is' homosexual, but the film offers no answers. What it does do, however, is very rigorously proscribe any sexual relation between Fergus and Dil. The sword of Damocles was never more effectively deployed than the blankets in the hotel on which Fergus lies and under which Dil sleeps, or the tightly-buttoned shirt and pants that Fergus never removes. The ambivalence which initially problematized the nature of gender concludes at one level by affirming the stability of a male performance, a performance displaced from the sexual register to that of 'caring'. In relation to this, Dil's own performance of the feminine is remarkably single-minded in its eliciting from Fergus a masculinity which he has not previously performed, even as a 'terrorist' (consider his violent protection of Dil from Dave or his defence of her 'honour' from the boss at the building site). The versions of femininity that Dil cites are almost entirely limited to those that transform the eliciting of desire into the impossible demand for care: 'The thing is, can you go the distance?' Dil's performance conforms precisely to the law of heterosexuality for which 'the desire of the woman is for the desire of the man', such that Fergus's relation to her is perfectly normative, if only to the degree that the corresponding 'desire of the man which is for the woman' can be suspended.[45] In this respect, for all its play with gender, the film plays to and reconfirms a heterosexual if not a necessarily masculine point of view, a view constantly assumed not only in the 'secrecy' which was demanded of the presumedly heterosexual critics and audiences of the film but in the 'uncanny' effect which that secrecy derives from the 'shock' of seeing Dil's sex: the effect expressed as 'Of course, I should have known', and which neatly mimes the structure of the oedipal complex within which what is seen must already have its place prescribed in order to be seen as significant at all. The film's erotic chasteness thus forcibly sublimates sexuality into care, effectively repeating the logic of the incest taboo which proscribes desire and instantiates the ethical subject through familial relations.[46]

We can, however, put a more problematic turn on Fergus's desire, a turn the film itself gestures to without 'going the distance'. This turn will require a remapping of the 'geography' of the film and a return to the field of ideology generally. The adequate image of the constraint that this entails, of the disavowal which permits the film's public success, is the glass wall that separates Fergus from Dil in the final prison scene. Titillating in its play with gender identity, the film is finally reassuring in enacting the most stringent taboos on queer sexuality. In effect, domestic harmony is performed by Fergus and Dil only where the state regulates their desire. A further 'improbability' is embedded in a remarkable disavowal of the actual conditions of Irish republican prisoners in British jails and of state policies designed to hinder family visitation, to separate prisoners from supportive communities and to criminalize rather than humanize political offenders.[47] In proceeding, I will seek to draw together the two plot elements which the film effectively disjoins, the romantic and the terrorist, in order that the potential crossings between them may be brought out.

Fergus's taking the rap for Dil represents both the authentication of Jody's diagnosis of his nature ('As the man said, it's in my nature') and the completion of the story which he began to tell for Jody but was unable to complete: Dil's 'You're doing time for me. No greater love, as the man says' picks up where Fergus's 'When I was a child . . . I thought as a child. But when I became a man I put away childish things . . .' left off. Her 'completion' of Fergus's truncated citation of St Paul by a further citation marks Fergus's passage to a 'mature' love of which, in his undeveloped terrorist incarnation, he was incapable. This love takes the form of taking responsibility protectively for an act which, according to the screenplay, Dil performs 'like a child, playing with a toy'. It can also be read as the redemption of a debt that Fergus owes to Jody although, as I should want to argue, only insofar as we recognize that Fergus's sense of debt precedes any that he might try to pay off by standing in for her man. But their performance of true love in a 'glass cage' is predicated upon the murder for which Fergus is doing time, that of Jude, the 'other woman' who threatens both Dil's 'femininity' and her possession of Fergus and Jody.

It has not often been noted that while Dil 'is' transvestite, it is Jude who most effectively performs femininity, and does so with a variety of which Dil seems not remotely capable. One might surmise that Jody's attraction to her, which succeeds in displacing Dil, is, as he suggests, not a matter of sexual preference – 'I didn't even fancy her' – or gender or, indeed, of race, but of a fascination with performance itself. Jude performs in succession a working-class and somewhat slatternly Irish lass, Fergus's movement girlfriend in an ethnically marked aran sweater, a hardened and heartless terrorist, an executive off the pages of *Vogue*, the jealous and jilted lover and, again, the hardened terrorist. More fascinating than the roles is the mobility of her transitions and her ability to play different registers:

(In the hostel)
She brings her lips close to his so they touch.
Jude: And I must admit I'm curious [about Dil].

He grabs her hair and pulls her head back.
Fergus: What the fuck do you know, Jude?
She pulls a gun and sticks it between his teeth.
Jude: You fucking tell me, boy —[48]

Her reappearance in this scene, and later in the hair salon and the Indian restaurant, doubles the uncanniness of seeing Dil's sex: the 'of course' which responds to her presence responds to her always already being there. The past that haunts Fergus is like a debt that always precedes him and shares the rhythms of the returns of the repressed. What I want to suggest is that Jude's interruptions of Fergus and Dil's intimacy function as a recurrent readmission of the violence that structures it, both in the sense of the larger social violence that produces and guarantees the sanctity of the domestic space and in that of the violence which gives way to the heterosexual relation. If, in Jordan's words, Dil 'represents the woman in all of us',[49] Jude figures not as the 'man in every woman', though that may be one of the effects of their doubling, but as trouble for representations of the feminine crucial to the heterosexual domestic space. She must, according to the narrative logic of the genre and of ideology, be violently removed.

In this, *The Crying Game* rejoins a constellation of recent films within which a terrorist threat to a domestic space must be met with violence and in which the violence of woman against woman is crucial. Let me cite here only two with which *The Crying Game* has fairly evident links and which are themselves interestingly intervolved, *Fatal Attraction* and *The Patriot Game*. *Fatal Attraction* famously involves an independent businesswoman (Glenn Close) who, in her obsession for Michael Douglas, becomes in effect a terrorist of his domestic space, stalking his wife (Ann Archer) and their daughter. Its climactic scene involves a peculiarly drawn-out fight between Ann Archer and Glenn Close, who has been concealed in the house, which is interrupted by Douglas, who apparently drowns Close in the bath. As he relaxes in nervous and physical exhaustion, Close suddenly rises from the bath to assault him yet again. At this moment, Ann Archer enters and shoots Close, who falls back against the wall leaving a bloody streak as she collapses to the ground. Others who know the film may have been struck by how the penultimate scene of *The Crying Game* enacts a virtual mirror image of that of the end of *Fatal Attraction*: where Ann Archer enters screen right to shoot Close, screen left, Dil appears screen left to shoot Jude, screen right; in both cases the apparently dead woman rises to be killed a second time; in both, the violence is woman on woman, while the male figure is effectively passive. In both, a peculiar pleasure seems to be derived from the drawn-out spectacle of the woman terrorist's bloody death. In both films, the death of the woman terrorist who is tied to the man's transgressive past allows for the possibility of a restoration of loving care between the couple. In both, murder is legitimate self-defence. In both, a profound misogyny is at play.

Fatal Attraction concludes with a lingering shot of a framed family photograph of Douglas, Archer and their daughter, as if recomposed after the terror has passed. *The Patriot Game* opens with a similar lingering pan around a room lined with such photographs only to cut to Ann Archer with her daughter in a hotel room in London where Tom Ryan (Harrison Ford) is lecturing the British Admiralty on the demise of the Soviet Fleet. Scarcely has this ex-CIA agent left the lecture hall than he intervenes to foil an Irish terrorist assassination attempt against members of the royal family. The consequence of this impulsive act is that one of the terrorists whose younger brother Ryan kills engages in an obsessive and vengeful pursuit of Ryan and his family, stalking and threatening their lives as Close does, and encroaching increasingly on their domestic space. One upshot of this threat is that Ryan returns to the CIA, deploying all the hi-tech capacities of the state in the attempt to expunge the terrorist splinter group, significantly training in Libya. But when this fails, it is once again Ann Archer who, in their besieged and invaded home, confronts and kills the woman terrorist who, the film has made clear, is the mastermind behind the group.

What I want to suggest by these allusions is that the figure of the terrorist-woman recurs in a transformed genre of terrorist film, not as the simple figure of domestic salvation, but as the aberrational figure that splits from proper femininity to threaten the well-regulated domestic space. This aberrational splitting of the feminine image legitimates the excessive violence that is required to expunge her.[50] The cinematic narrative that opens the possibility of non-normative gender roles is obliged violently to close off those possibilities. If, as Tom Laqueur has suggested, *The Crying Game* is the story of a penis out of place,[51] that story at the level of anatomical sex distinction is powerfully contained by the stabilization of gender relations around heterosexual norms, to the extent that the woman out of place, which is the other story, must encounter a bloody come-uppance. At this point, the gender politics of the film, which ultimately appear to make it playful and comforting rather than disturbing to norms, rejoins the liberal narrative of counter-insurgency. For intrinsic to the criminalizing logic of counter-insurgency, as we have been seeing throughout, is the representation of terrorism as a threat to domestic security and the characterization of the terrorists as pathological and hypermasculine 'men of violence'. Crucial to this set of representations, especially within the liberal imaginary to which a film like *The Crying Game* speaks, is the understanding of insurgency as repressively and atavistically masculine or patriarchal and correspondingly destructive of a femininity generally associated with motherhood and passivity. Within such terms, it is impossible that a feminist project should be linked to violence or that a woman could find in armed struggle a legitimate locus of agency: the complexity of activists like Mairead Farrell becomes virtually unthinkable; Jude can only be a virago or a bitch.[52]

From this perspective, it is Jude rather than Dil who represents the film's locus of maximum instability: she marks, as her name suggests, the treacherous ground where the essentialist stereotypes of gender are forced into their point of ambivalence. For the woman terrorist figures and 'blows up' the moment in the logic of gender where the seductions of beauty coalesce with the terror of the sublime.[53] Occupying the place that is designated to that of 'men of violence', Jude in fact represents an incipient violence and threat already predicated on the feminine, according to a set of stereotypes that operates in both the 'universal' dimension of the Medusa and the specifically Irish domain that we saw invoked in *The Green Flag*. The universal register of the stereotype may mark precisely the instability or ambivalence that arises from the location of 'woman' on the borderlines of nature and culture or of life and death, but the specifically Irish resonances open a slightly different set of disturbances which the film sets in motion but can neither fully contain nor fully entertain.

For, in the long history of stereotypes about the Irish, a peculiar conjuncture persists which combines violence with femininity. Arnold's famously 'feminine' Celt is simultaneously turbulent, titanic and ungovernable.[54] The association of violence, femininity and ungovernability designates, of course, precisely what Jude embodies: a feminine which is at once out of place, exceeding the boundaries of the domestic space on which governmentality relies, and unregulated, excessive, and treacherously seductive. *The Crying Game*, at the level of its narrative resolutions, confirms this stereotype. But if we follow through the lines of disturbance which it registers and evokes to the point to which it does not go, the outlines of another narrative emerge. This would mean pursuing the convergence between the racial narrative about Ireland and the gender stereotypes which alternatively parallel and displace it in the film, recognizing that the racial narratives are already gendered.

The Crying Game teases us with the question as to what kind of a woman Dil is while in a sense endowing Jude with all the attributes of phallic power and of feminine masquerades. But what kind of a man is Fergus, whose most singular attribute might seem to be his delicious passivity and his bewildered self-consciousness about the roles he performs both as terrorist and as heterosexual lover? We discover Dil to be a woman who happens to have a penis; is there anything within the laws of verisimilitude of this film to suggest to us that Fergus is not a man who happens not to have a penis? This is no more than a literalization of what is apparent throughout the film, his perpetual inadequacy in relation to the roles he is called on to perform, terrorist killer or 'man': this Fergus whom Jody describes as the one with 'the baby face' is far from being in possession of the phallus. The anxiety caused by such an ineluctable inadequacy determines the iterative performance of heterosexual identity as perpetually shaded with a melancholy that its normalization belies.[55] *The Crying Game* struggles to overcome the spectacle of inadequacy and the shades of melancholy in the same moment, the film's conclusion. Here Fergus appears to have succeeded in finding a way to pay the debt which has always haunted him and in doing so to become the man he never was:

that is, both a Man and Dil's man. And all in the name of the shadowy figure of the man whom they cite:

> Dil: . . . You're doing time for me. No greater love, as the man says. Wish you'd tell me why.
> Fergus: As the man said, it's in my nature.
> CAMERA PULLS BACK, and as Fergus tells the story of the scorpion and the frog, the music comes up – 'Stand By Your Man'.[56]

According to the film's ostensible narrative, Fergus becomes a man, maturing away from the 'childish things' of his Irish past as he 'does time'.[57] But the time he does has already been done before the imprisonment. Assuming the role of Dil's protector, he is at once man and father; leaving behind the atavisms of the Irish terrorist, he assumes his fuller humanity as a properly gendered subject. What the redundancy of the prison sentence evokes is not the need of further reform, but the rigour by which heterosexuality must be preserved, in the strictly Lacanian sense, as the absence of sexual relation. Like every comedy, the laughter is shadowed by the melancholy of the perpetually missed encounter.

So, in the end, the full exercise of the violence of the state is called on to maintain the film's comic and finally heterosexual resolution.[58] What it precludes is at once a sexual and a racial encounter along lines that do not follow the trajectory of modernity by which, in his passage from premodern Ireland to postmodern London, Fergus becomes humanized. To do so demands asking the question that the film itself raises but does not pursue: why are Jody and Dil 'black'? And why, as black characters, are they in their different ways, like Fergus, not quite men? We recall Fanon's polemical statement, 'The black man is not a man', and the ambiguities which haunt and explain it: 'man' is both a gender category and one which designates adequacy to human 'species being'. With regard to both categories, the Irishman and his black counterpart under colonialism are found wanting. The universal trajectory of modernity proposes, asymptotically, to resolve their double inadequacy.[59]

But suppose we start to tell the story differently, against the grain of historiographical and cinematic verisimilitude, so that Dil and Fergus do not step back into their assigned places in the social order of modernity. This would involve our tracking, not the incompletion of Irish culture with regard to modernity or the aberrations of Irish gender and sexuality in relation to modernity's norms, but rather the singular history of bodies and cultures formed and transformed on the borders where modernity always emerges in disjunction with, and mutually informed by, the non-modern. It would involve elaborating further the space of the colonized body, at once hypermasculinized and feminized, and the violence which founds the state and the systems of gender and social distribution of spaces that at different moments it entails. Above all, it involves thinking along the conflicted borders, or the interface between incommensurable spaces, that nonetheless interact and transform one another: the perpetual instability of these spaces denies their historian the steadiness of paradigms or the assurance of a grammar with which he or she is placed as subject.

To such a trajectory *The Crying Game* gestures; from it, it turns away, finding the only possible resolution of its flirtations with non-identity to lie in the re-establishment of the laws of gender and the sanctioning of state violence. The generic haven of comedy – the restoration of a modified patriarchal law after all the mistaken identities and troubled boundaries are fixed – is where the film finds its home. Hence, for all the film's improbabilities, the deep sigh of satisfied verisimilitude with which it ends. The common sense of eternal verities, of 'human nature', has been stretched and teased but yet maintains its sway. In this, it accords with the pattern of dominant historical narrative: even in the device that resolves the drama lies the projection of a mythic Medusa, Jude, whose anti-social, anti-domestic drives must be annihilated. In both genres of narrative, common sense outlaws and targets the myth that is its own projection. In this sense, then, the myths of history and of conventional narrative fictions are the requisite agency of hegemony, as 'tradition' was for modernity or atavistic violence for the state. Counter to many accounts of hegemony, including Gramsci's own, this suggests that in fact myth, folklore, common sense and ideology are not each other's doubles: myth and folklore are not simply sedimented popular versions of outmoded philosophies, but function, rather, as the names and screens affixed by historians in those openings where there might be a way into alternative logics of time and space. As Ashis Nandy has powerfully argued, a different conception of myth functions athwart modernity to offer the possibility of a less determining relation to the past.[60] Given that they are embedded in the material effects of colonial modernity itself, there is nothing mystifying about these other histories: the historian needs only to learn to think awry.

OUTSIDE HISTORY
Irish New Histories and the 'Subalternity Effect'

I

Recent shifts in Irish historiography align some of its practitioners, implicitly if not programmatically, with the kinds of questioning that have been associated with the Indian subaltern historians. The implications of such historical work for Irish cultural studies are both timely and far-reaching, focusing our attention on how the study of subaltern groups in Ireland, as elsewhere, has entailed a critique of the 'modernizing' or enlightenment assumptions that structure a state formation largely inherited from British imperial institutions. At the same time, criticisms of the critique of enlightenment have also emerged, particularly from feminist perspectives, which demand that we nuance the kinds of exploration that may be undertaken under the rubrics of subalternity or 'postcolonialism'.

The apparent familiarity of Irish discussions in the larger context of subaltern historiography derives not from any given analogies between Irish and Indian history or historiography (though at some level of analysis such analogies may certainly be maintained) but from the regularity of what we might call a 'subalternity effect' in colonial spaces.[1] That is, the social space of the 'subaltern' designates not some sociological datum of an objective and generalizable kind, but is an effect emerging in and between historiographical discourses. As we have seen in earlier chapters, both the terms 'postcolonial' and 'subaltern' designate in different but related ways the desire to elaborate social spaces which are recalcitrant to any straightforward absorption – ever more inevitable though this often seems – of Ireland into European modernity. There is, however, no simple retrieval of occluded social formations and practices within either set of projects. The return to the archive by and large involves the historian in the recovery of silhouettes that rise up on the horizon of official discourse – in police archives, in ethnographic works, in bureaucratic reports or philanthropic appeals. Such glimpses register the porous limits of official history and, for the contemporary materialist, furnish the archaeological fragments that suggest as much the necessity of a critique as definite contours for a positive historical reconstruction of the past. To reiterate an earlier point, the shadow play of alternative histories marks the limit of the state and of official historiography as their reversion to material and epistemological violence. But this perpetual and catastrophic return of the limit appears to us now so constant a manifestation of historical representation and state practice that we can say that the historical state formation continually produces subaltern spaces not as facts that it can grasp but as effects that escape it. As *constitutive* effects of historical rationality, subaltern spaces do not mark a deconstructive *mise-en-abîme* of historical consciousness, as Gayatri Spivak has suggested.[2] They are, rather, as the chapters 'Nationalisms against the State' and 'Regarding Ireland in a Postcolonial Frame' argued, constituent elements of colonial modernity and agencies in, rather than passive objects of, state formation. Their rhythms of transformation are accordingly those of their survival, their living on 'after history', but in a continuing differential relation to modernity.

What these considerations suggest, then, is a double sense in which, as effects, subaltern formations are performative. They are so in that their articulation, in practice and in memory, brings into being new states of culture and practice, whether in the transformation of modern legal structures or in the emergence of new modes of non-modern recalcitrance. Furthermore, though, the historical representation of their continuity as *discontinuous*, as sporadic, is the symptom of the unanticipated directions that subaltern formations take below the horizon of official history. Their recurrence, or 'iteration', each time anew, introduces a deviation into the time-line of the state: the swerve that results from the invocation of the apparently past in a new place displaces historical determination and makes way for alternative cultural logics. We may invoke here Raymond Williams's useful triadic structure of terms for the temporality of cultural struggles – the residual, the dominant and the emergent – and yet rewrite them.[3] For it is not, in the context of capitalist colonialism, that the 'residual' would denote a reactive resistance to the dominant state and its cultural hegemony; instead, the residual, made invisible except as atavism and myth to official discourse, recurs as the *emergent* form of newly antagonistic practices. This rhythm of return is that of the survival of alternative social imaginations amid the ruins of shattered cultures and the traces of state violence.

In the following sections, a repertoire of alternative historical possibilities will emerge from a review of the various directions and debates in Irish historiography. This will involve drawing together the documentary recovery of formerly little examined spaces with the performative dimensions of opening up the historical field itself.

II

Ranajit Guha, in his well-known preface to *Subaltern Studies*,[4] projects subaltern historiography as the elaboration of occluded spaces, constituted ambiguously by previous modes of historiography and/or by the statist orientation of colonial and nationalist politics as marginal. The élite histories of imperialists, nationalists and Marxists alike are displaced by the subaltern's inquiry into peasant movements, the anomalies of proletarian formation in India, and so forth. In this sense, the preface partially follows its ostensible mentor, Antonio Gramsci, in understanding the intimate relation between élite historiography and the state formation. In another sense, as I have argued in the chapter 'Nationalisms against the State', the subaltern project thus described deviates significantly from Gramsci's Hegelian Marxist one in refusing to reinscribe the end of subalternity in the capture of the state. No less than Indian historiography, the course of Irish history writing has been bound to state formations. Irish cultural nationalism from the 1840s on turns around the contestation of a Whig historiography for which Ireland's successive civil struggles culminated in its benevolent absorption into the British constitution. But nationalist historians, lacking Gramsci's elegant interpretation of their quite typical dilemma, were unable to produce Irish history without remarking constantly on its peculiarly *discontinuous* narrative, on its untotalizable tale of spasmodic uprisings and defeats or its 'fragmentary and episodic' cultural forms. As Gramsci might have predicted, only the admittedly partial capture of an independent state ushers in the heyday of nationalist histories whose teleological version of the Irish national struggle became the staple of the national curriculum. To quote from one such text, Edmund Curtis's standard *History of Ireland*, first published in 1936:

> To make a country's history intelligible, the historian naturally seeks for some point of unity, and this has been long deferred in Ireland's history . . . For the establishment of a central government representing the nation and able to rule justly over all its elements, Ireland has had to wait till the present generation.[5]

Since then, however, Irish historiography has not followed the pattern ascribed by Guha to Indian historiography. For the contestation of nationalist histories, until relatively recently, came not from anything akin to either Marxist or subaltern studies but rather from a large and impressive body of historical work which has become known as 'revisionist history'.[6] The focus of this work has been less on the epic of national struggle and more on the emergence under British administration of modern state institutions in Ireland: the national education system, national police force, the legal apparatus and so forth. Though it has perhaps been superseded as a standard text by R. F. Foster's *Modern Ireland, 1600–1972* (1989), F. S. L. Lyons's *Ireland since the Famine* (1971) is still a summary instance of the tendencies of this group of historians, synthesizing into a larger narrative much of the work on nineteenth- and twentieth-century institution building that had been produced in individual monographs. The methodological as well as political underpinnings of this historiography are inextricable from the consolidation in Ireland of institutions of higher education: the revisionist emphasis on the emergence of modern state institutions as the proper object of history nicely exemplifies how the material conditions of disciplines are repeated in their discursive formations. Indeed, the supercession of an avowedly political nationalist historiography by a professionalized and empirically sceptical methodology occurred for the most part through the prior retraining of Irish historians in British institutions.[7]

In the wake of a still dominant 'revisionist' history, Irish historiography has yet to produce anything as self-conscious and theoretically reflective as *Subaltern Studies*. Nevertheless, it is clear that the last fifteen years or so has seen the emergence of a large corpus of non-élite histories: histories of agrarian movements, local histories, social histories of the complex intersections of class and colonization in rural Ireland, women's history, in the form both of biographical work and, more recently, of studies of women's movements and social history. The historiographical influences and analogues of these studies have been various, but include in particular the 'history from below' of Thompson and Hobsbawm or the social and gender history of journals like *History Workshop* on the one hand, and French every-day and local histories on the other. It would thus be wrong to seek to homogenize either the impulses behind or the products of the new Irish histories.[8]

The cumulative effect of this historical work, however, has been to shift significantly the narrative axes of Irish history. The concentration of nationalist and revisionist historiography on state seizure and state building is displaced by histories (the plural is deliberate) whose narrative telos has ceased to be the state. As we have seen, the 'ends' of the Irish labour movement have not been, nor were ever assumed to be, coincident with the foundation of the Irish state. The same holds true for the various movements for women's emancipation that have emerged since the mid-nineteenth century: it is probably no accident that the major feminist contributions to Irish history of the last decade have been biographies of the principal women figures of the first quarter of this century whose active involvement in the national, labour and women's movements issued in their corresponding opposition to the conservative Catholic state that actually came into existence. For it is precisely the inadequacy of the organizing narrative of state formation to represent such struggles, and the failure of the state itself to respond even to that dimension of feminist and labour demands whose expression takes shape within the forms of legal discourses on rights and citizenship, that has required the opening of further studies in the longer duration of labour and women's history. What such studies may yet clarify is the extent to which the failures of the state lie in the peculiar conjunction of modernity and non-modernity that forms the cultural substrate of the post-1922 Irish states. To the implications of such contradictory formations for the understanding of a gender history of Ireland we will return later.

III

But it is at this point that the political and epistemological significance, if that distinction still has any meaning, of invoking Ireland's *postcolonial* status and the performative nature of historical discourse, including that of subalternity, becomes manifest. For the *anticolonial* nature of the Irish nationalist struggle is not expressed through any 'objective' decision as to the political status of Ireland within the United Kingdom or the British Empire. It is located rather in the peculiarity, within the Western European frame, or the typicality, within the context of global anti-colonial struggles, of Irish nationalism's appeal to its premodernity as the site of significant cultural differences on which to found a distinct but no less *modern* state formation, equivalent to if not identical with that of Britain. Or, to put it differently, Irish nationalism appealed to the very characteristics which were, to imperial eyes, the marks of the people's underdevelopment and inherent dependence to provide the grounds of its claim to independence. The state is, accordingly, founded upon a fetishization of invented traditions which are constitutively rather than contingently (as might be argued for the 'traditions' of metropolitan states) in contradiction to the state's need to form abstract political subjects as citizens. Many of the social contradictions that have attended Ireland's entry into the European Community circulate around this ideological necessity by which the state was constituted around a conservative cultural identity whose traditionalism conflicts with concepts of abstract individual rights which are fundamental to the idea of the modern state. One favoured resolution of this contradiction, at one with attempts elsewhere in Europe to subsume and pre-empt possible minority or national insurgencies, has been sought in the EC policy of regionalism. This policy, which has been much espoused by the social democratic nationalist John Hume, has the absurd goal of preserving cultural difference within the broader plan for rationalizing and homogenizing the European political economy.[9] It is, in other words, a merely aesthetic response to the contradictions of modernization and cultural difference.

The conclusion to be drawn from these observations is not, however, that Ireland accordingly must be seen to have undergone a so far incomplete modernization, as if modernity had some discernible if Platonic ideal as its telos.[10] On the contrary, we can recognize that the form in which Ireland entered its modernity was constitutively contradictory, on both sides of the border. One of the most striking symptoms of Ireland's colonial history is the virtually chiasmic relation between the two post-Treaty states: where the Republic constituted itself around conservative traditionalism in order to forge a modern democratic state, Northern Ireland sought to legitimate its separation by appeal to the values of civil society. Yet, since these values were explicitly derived from Protestantism, this appeal succeeded in constituting a violently sectarian state.[11] Not untypical of the dynamic of colonial history generally, this instance of contradictory modernity helps us to trouble the distinction usually made, and constantly invoked in Irish debates, between the matrix of modernity, state institutions, rationality and historiography itself, on the one hand, and that of traditionalism, tribalism or localism, irrationality and mythology on the other. For if the state relies, in the postcolonial moment, on the canonization of a certain selection of practices then termed tradition, and forges that canon through nationalist histories, it relies equally on a violence proportional in intensity and kind to the resistance it meets in order to repress or erase the traces of other practices and narratives. In Northern Ireland, that violence has been constantly manifest in the massive deployment since 1922 of sectarian repressive state apparatuses sanctioned by permanent emergency laws; in the Republic, the violence has been mostly a function of the ideological state apparatuses, due initially to de Valera's successful incorporation of political opposition to the Free State and constantly to the safety valve of massive emigration.

Cliona Murphy has remarked that 'The controversy regarding revisionism in Irish history is ironic considering the narrowness of the history that has been at the centre of the dispute – nationalist history.'[12] While the focus of both nationalist history and revisionism has been on nation-state formation, with a shift of focus from heroes to bureaus, the multiple foci of the new histories have been on the sites and narratives which the state formation constitutively occludes. The shift of focus entails equally the production of different subjects and different temporalities while simultaneously bringing into play the ideological location of the historian. As Murphy herself points out, the very project of women's history, even before the question of a specifically feminist perspective, questions not only the contents of previous histories and their principally male protagonists, but also the institutional construction of objectivity: what is objective is not merely a function of empirical method but is bound to the modes of narrative verisimilitude which, as with the literary canon, divide significant from insignificant, major from minor subjects. Crucial to the self-evidences of historiography, as she elsewhere points out, is the normativity of historical 'periods'.[13] To take up an earlier point, women's history in Ireland, as elsewhere, has had to move gradually from studies devoted to figures made prominent by their relation to concerns of the state – i.e. nationalists and suffragists – to studies increasingly devoted to the 'daily life' of women in Ireland, as if the former studies legitimated the latter.[14] A not dissimilar set of observations about the institutional construction of histories that matter can be made in relation to the recent upsurge of local histories, many if not most of which have been undertaken by non-professional historians, or by academics from other disciplines. In this case also, the subjects of history, in the sense of its writers as of its agents, have changed, together with implicit assumptions as to both what counts as history and what historical processes 'seem like'.[15]

The shifts in perspective that the new histories imply are numerous, and akin to many with which readers of subaltern histories will be familiar.

Among these might be included a rethinking of popular culture, not in terms of tradition or its 'betrayal', but in terms of its capacity to conjoin processes of adaptation and resistance (the refunctioning of printed ballads or of melodramas – commodity forms principally emanating from Britain – for political agitation being but two instances); the study of social formations which proved insusceptible to absorption into the state formation or the nationalist movements which shaped it (such as the agrarian movements of the eighteenth and nineteenth centuries and the short-lived soviets of the 1920s); the examination of the ways in which the daily lives, especially of working-class women, cut across the neat division of gendered social spheres on which the Republic's constitution itself is founded.[16]

In each of the above instances, what is troubled is not merely a set of assumptions as to the 'proper' content or object of history, but its narrative ends. Popular culture can no longer be seen in relation to a putative adherence to or deviation from a resurgence of national consciousness embodied in traditions, nor can its insurgencies be seen merely as, in Hobsbawm's terms, 'proto-nationalist', awaiting their full significance in absorption into the nationalist struggle for the state.[17] Whether we are speaking of agrarian struggles, women's history or of non-élite cultural forms, what this implies is the recalcitrance of each of these historical sites to the formation of abstract political subjectivity in which, for all its ideological traditionalism, official Irish nationalism conjoins with the project of modernity. At the same time, however, it is equally impossible to narrate the histories of non-élite social and cultural formations in abstraction from the narrative of state formation. For the latter narrative certainly relates, from the perspective of state and modernity, the story of successive attempts to incorporate recalcitrant formations, implying that the history of non-élite formations is always at least partially the history of their constitution and emergence as resistant, if not always openly, to state formation. I emphasize this in order to insist again on the *contemporaneity* of non-élite formations to those which are taken by élite historiography to represent modern forms which supersede outmoded or primitive 'traditions': as responses of adjustment and resistance to the 'modern' social transformations whose institutions they may often have provoked, they constitute spaces adjacent rather than 'prior' to the state formation itself.

It is in this sense that we can begin to comprehend a phenomenon which we might term 'oscillation' that Luke Gibbons captures so well in reference to popular understandings of traditional ballads like 'The Lass of Aughrim'. Discussing this and similar ballads, Gibbons points to the difficulty of knowing when such a figure is to be seen as an individual and historical person and when as a refunctioning of traditional allegories.[18] The oscillation between allegorical and historical interpretations of the lass takes place precisely in the shift of social location that the interpreting subject at any given moment occupies. The fading of the allegorical mode of understanding is a function of the accession of the subject to the symbolic modes proper to the representative histories of the nation-state formation. But it is important to stress that it is a fading which takes place in time with the emergence of a dominant social narrative and from the latter's perspective: the space occupied by the non-élite social formation is occluded rather than erased or superseded by the dominant and persists even in that occlusion. Rey Ileto's work on the Philippine bandits has already been instructive to us and it remains important not to dissolve the formal discontinuity emblematized by the bandit (or, in the Irish context, agrarian movements or women's culture, for example) in emphasizing their 'always already thereness'. Constituted in simultaneity with, and difference from, modern civil society, and representing in a certain sense the 'constitutive other' of modernity, these spaces that are the object of 'new histories' are not, we have argued, to be conceived as alternative continuities, parallel to dominant narratives and only awaiting, in Gramsci's sense, to attain hegemony in order to be completed. On the contrary, and at the risk of deliberate hypostasization, the apparent discontinuity of popular or non-élite history furnishes indications of alternative social formations, difficult as these may be to document and decipher for the disciplined historian; the same discontinuity as well as the formal grounds for the persistent inassimilability of non-élite formations to the state.

Of course, the *sporadic* appearance of popular resistance is always in part a function of the historians' own perspectives, but I would argue, if tentatively, for the more substantive claim that popular memory constitutes a repertoire of narratives, mythemes, rumours, retained and reconstellated, that flash up, like Benjamin's dialectical images, in moments of danger.[19] Like Benjamin's image, the constellations of popular memory are spatial more than temporal formations, whose very 'failure' to totalize and whose formal hybridity allow for the accommodation of multiple locations among which the non-élite subject oscillates. Among those locations are those sites in which that subject is indeed interpellated, if incompletely, as citizen-subject. The insubordination of such formations is in precise differentiation to the narrative forms of official histories.[20] For the latter, faced with the impossibility of totalizing societies whose mode of rationalization is simultaneously and paradoxically disintegrative and homogenizing, endow totality with a narrative structure which, though never itself finally closed, continually subordinates inassimilable social groups to the status of the prerational and primitive. The recurrent insurgence of those groups correspondingly appears as sporadic and irrational violence and as an index of the failure of Irish society, in this instance, to have fully emerged into modernity. It is the implicit and explicit project, on the other hand, of postcolonial, subaltern or simply 'new' histories to open the spaces within which unsubordinated narratives can resonate. That resonance is the effect of the excess of possible histories, subject positions, affects, affiliations or memories over the singular history through which the state seeks to incorporate and regulate its political subjects.

IV

The position on modernity and the state formation that I have been drawing out of the Irish new histories has been contested from a number of positions, of which the feminist version is the most complex. Such critiques generally have a dual focus: on the one hand, on the conservatism of both Irish states, on the other, the presumed conservatism of Irish communities. Although the former focus targets appropriately the deployment of tradition and sectarianism respectively by hegemonic state nationalisms, the latter focus firstly presumes the accuracy of representations of Irish communities as conservative and secondly misreads what I would term the *performative* intervention of the critique of modernity.[21]

One effect of the new histories has been to challenge both the assumption of the inherent conservatism of the Irish populace and that of the traditionalism of Irish republicanism in general, assumptions that structure, to different ends, both nationalist and revisionist historiographies. As one of two salient instances, the longstanding understanding of the 1798 uprising as resulting from an incongruous alliance between enlightened and mostly middle-class Protestant republicans on the one hand and a traditionally-minded Gaelic and Catholic peasantry on the other has recently begun to crumble. This has happened on account of new research not only on the social composition of the 'peasant' rebels but also on intellectual contacts, through priests and school-teachers, between Ireland and the Continent outside élite circles.[22] The implications of this research may well be carried forward to new understandings of subaltern radicalism through the nineteenth century and into the post-independence period.

A second instance of the questioning of assumptions involves continuing research on the effects of emigration on the social and political composition of rural Ireland during the post-Famine consolidation of larger landholdings. This consolidation enabled the emergence of what Emmet Larkin referred to as the 'nation-building class', the small farmers. The relation between this class and the social and cultural conservatism of the Irish nationalism that founded the Irish Free State in 1922 is not difficult to find, but cannot be extended to Irish society as a whole.[23] As the historian Joseph Lee has recently been arguing, the apparent relative economic and political success of Ireland with regard to other decolonizing societies must necessarily be understood in relation to decades of emigration, which have maintained Irish population levels at around five million rather than the fourteen million that might have been reasonably projected at the moment of independence. Given that circumstance, the degree of Ireland's continuing structural dependence and underdevelopment becomes all the more remarkable even as the social stability of the Republic becomes more explicable, for reasons indicated above. Again, despite the predominant image of the Irish male emigrant, recent research indicates that the impact of emigration may have been greater on Irish women than on

Irish men, although partially disguised by the vocational nature of much female emigration: missionary, educational and nursing work dominating alongside domestic service.[24]

The patriarchal conservatism of the post-independence state accordingly needs to be understood in terms of a longer history involving at least three factors: the pre-independence class formations that brought bourgeois nationalism into dominance, the contradictions of post-1920s populism through which de Valera gained and maintained power despite the often socially disastrous effects of his isolationist economic policies, and the persisting importance of emigration as the means to maintaining social and economic stability by diffusing conflict. In the light of such histories, it might become apparent that, however paradoxically, a socially conservative or 'traditionalist' state was the instrument by which post-independence Ireland negotiated its entry into global capitalism and modernity. In a certain sense, this very paradox permitted Ireland's rapid transition through the 1960s and 1970s from an isolated economy to a classic instance of 'dependence': the depletion of organized labour and the 'traditionally' highly-gendered division of labour furnished ideal conditions for multi-national corporate investment akin to those of other postcolonial nations but advantageously located within the European Community. The impact of the cycle of state-subsidized foreign investment in largely assembly-oriented industry, short-term surplus-value extraction and subsequent plant closure has been especially severe on a predominantly female workforce in a fashion strikingly correspondent to the situation of women elsewhere within the larger structures of post-Fordist global capitalism.[25] And, as in those other locations, the Irish postcolonial state's sponsorship of traditionalist social relations, especially in the domain of gender relations, has contributed substantially to the possibility of hyperexploitation of labour in general and women's labour in particular at the present.[26]

Currently, the increasing integration of Ireland within the political and legal as well as economic framework of the European Community is accentuating the contradictions between the state's traditional ideology and its modernizing forms. The European Court at Strasbourg offers a court of appeal for civil liberties beyond the Irish (and, it must be noted, British) courts. In this respect, Europe certainly has offered the possibility of extending the realization of those civil rights promised by the modern political state into domains of the family and sexuality where they had largely been denied, both by the Irish constitution, as in the case of abortion and divorce, and by related legislation. Accordingly, the apparent completion of a project of modernity and the full extension of rights of citizenship are linked in the struggle against patriarchal conservatism. As Clara Connolly put it in her review of recent Irish critiques of the universalism of Western modernity:

> We know that all over the contemporary world, these notions [of abstract humanity] are being replaced by the most frightening forms of communalism,

and 'difference'-based ethnic exclusivism. In that scenario, women are merely the property of the group, the symbol of the nation's future, to be protected or defiled according to their belonging. The concept of equality enshrined in 'citizenship' offers more to women than that.[27]

Within the limits of a liberal agenda that practically imposes itself on the activist, the appeal to universal abstract rights is opposed to communal particularism. But it is just that, an abstraction that cannot take into account the complex eddies of citizen formation in the postcolonial state. The long history of modernity and of nationalism in Ireland has not involved any simple opposition between abstract universalism and reactionary particularism. On the contrary, as much of the new history is already demonstrating, each enfolds the other while producing contemporaneous and resistant alternatives. That is, the universalizing project of imperial modernity, so well detailed in much revisionist history, is at one with the needs of nationalism to produce the modern citizen-subject as the subject of the nation-state. Hence the assiduous preservation of the apparatuses, ideological and repressive, of the British state after 1922. At the same time, that state nationalism has redeployed ideas of tradition and racial stereotypes that were equally crucial to the maintenance of an imperial discourse on modernity and identity, redefining them only to mark its difference within the same forms. The consequence has been an effort, common to imperialism and the national state, to marginalize inassimilable and recalcitrant social groups, cultural forms and political projects.

Nowhere has this been more apparent than in the complex history of gender in Ireland. Briefly, since the history of gender relations in modern Ireland has only recently begun to emerge, Irish nationalism and British imperialism largely concur in the late nineteenth century in associating self-government and 'manliness', at the level of the individual person as at that of the nation. In reaction to 'celticist' stereotypes of the 'feminine Celt' produced by Matthew Arnold and others, Irish nationalism reacts by seeking to produce a rigorous re-engendering of social spaces in Ireland, culminating in the Constitution of 1937 with its explicit division of masculine and feminine spheres. The process is clearly analogous to processes which Ashis Nandy has described within the Indian context in The Intimate Enemy. That project, however, would appear to have worked against the grain of Irish sociality and to have failed to grasp the social and economic consequences of imperialism. For the stereotype of Irish 'femininity' is not merely an invention, but is a refraction into terms that legitimate empire of what must have been marked differences in the codings of gender, its economic and social significance, and the articulation of affect, or what Williams has termed 'structures of feeling'.[28] At the same time, given the terms of Victorian and modern constructions of gender, the structural position of Irish males, as dispossessed and disenfranchised, corresponds in part to the position generally designated feminine, while few Irish women have ever simply occupied domestic spaces. The contradiction between the assumptions and project of the modern state, as indeed of capitalist gender relations, and the historical and material conditions of Irish men and women has been profoundly productive of anomic masculinity in Ireland. What has yet to be adequately documented and analysed is the emergence of differently articulated male and female homosocial spheres in colonial and postcolonial Ireland, though these doubtless exist and have probably profoundly affected political and social life in Ireland. It is an open question whether these spheres will appear to historical research merely as effects of colonial damage or as resources for alternative visions of cultural and social life.

The consideration that in fact social forms regarded as damaged, whether from a perspective that sees them as remnants or residues of past forms or from one that sees them as inadequately developed, may nonetheless represent resources for alternative projects is fundamental to the possibilities I am still seeking to draw from Irish subaltern historiography. The implication of the new Irish histories is that the resistances inscribed in non-élite histories represent, not a mere adherence to often outmoded cultural traditions, but sites of a complex intersection of individual and communal locations which resist reduction to the form of civil subjectivity which dominant narratives prioritize. The *performativity* that I seek to draw from this currently fluid and by no means integrated body of researches involves the attempt to produce and theorize dialectically out of such materials the possibility that social and cultural forms which are necessarily relegated to residual status by dominant historiography might generate forms for emergent practices, even where their apparent content may be in some views simply conservative. Where the emancipatory claims of both nationalism and Marxism have been predicated effectively on the need to erase and surpass contemporary social and cultural forms and to seek the resources for social transformation in a dialectical relation to the deep past, it may yet be possible to locate in the marginalized forms of lived social relations the contours of radical imaginaries. The insistence of the new histories on the *contemporaneity* of marginal and dominant social forms, and on their differential construction, is in this respect a profoundly instructive corrective to the self-evidences of developmental historiographies which over and again relegate difference to anteriority.

THE RECOVERY OF KITSCH

An irrepressible conundrum mocks national cultures, all the more so when, overshadowed by more powerful neighbours, culture is all the nation has to distinguish it. That conundrum is the apparently inevitable declension of the icons of authentic national culture into kitsch. The images proliferate: round towers and wolfhounds, harps and shamrocks, la Virgen de Guadalupe and pyramids in Yucatan, Aztec masks and feathered serpents. And they have their histories, disinterred and shaped in the projects of cultural nationalism to symbolize the primordial origins of the spirit of the nation, *la raza*. But long before their visible commodification as signals of safe exoticism deployed by our tourist boards, breweries or airlines, the logic of their standardization and circulation was embedded in the nationalist project.

What does cultural nationalism want? In the first place, to retrieve for the people an authentic tradition that, in its primordiality and continuity, differentiates the nation culturally if not racially from those that surround or occupy it. This act of retrieval seeks to reroot the cultural forms that have survived colonization in the deep history of a people and to oppose them to the hybrid and grafted forms that have emerged in the forced mixing of cultures that colonization entails. It is an archaeological and genealogical project aimed at purification and refinement, at originality and authenticity. The fact that, as we know only too well, most tradition is invented tradition is less significant than the act of resistant self-differentiation that this project involves.

For, in the second place, it is to identify with this difference that cultural nationalism calls its prospective subjects. Rather than masquerading as a well-formed Anglo or Englishman, celebrate our differences, even where they are marked as signs of inferiority. Transvalue the values of the colonizer, cease to defer to the dominant culture and its commodities, produce and consume authentic national goods. Above all, cultivate the sentiment of a difference that unifies the people against the colonizing power, for in that sentiment of difference survives the spirit of the nation. Cultural nationalism seeks accordingly to reform the structures of feeling of individuals, emancipating their affects from dependence and inferiority and directing them towards an independence founded in cultural integrity. It must do so by deploying artefacts that are the symbols of national culture, parts which represent a whole that is often yet to be constituted: ballads or corridas, myths, tales, poetry, music and costumes, murals. Around these, the sentiment of national culture is to be forged in each and every individual.

To achieve these ends, cultural nationalists must deploy, in the name of tradition itself, the most modern techniques of reproduction and dissemination.

Benedict Anderson has noted the importance of the press, and its commodity forms, the newspaper and the novel, to the emergence of nationalism.[1] We can extend the sweep of nationalism's dependence on the circulation of cultural commodities to include forms from the street ballad, cheaply produced and disseminated by pedlars, to radio, television and cinema. Nationalist sentiment is borne by commodities whose circulation encompasses the whole national territory. And if every corner of the prospective nation is washed by this circulation, so too each individual must be saturated with the same sentiment, without which the uniformity and unity of popular political desire could not be forged. Cultural nationalism requires a certain homogenization of affect, a requirement served not so much by selection as by proliferation, the dissemination of countless ballads, newspaper articles, symbols and images which are virtually indistinguishable. Indeed, a considerable degree of stylistic uniformity, a simulacrum of the anonymity of 'folk' artefacts, is indispensable to the project: stylistic idiosyncracy would be counter-productive; stylization is of the essence.

Hence the apparent inevitability of the devolution of 'authentic national culture' into kitsch. The commodification of certain styles and the mechanical reproduction of standardized forms of affect that have traditionally been the hallmarks of kitsch have their close counterparts in cultural nationalism. Only here the reproduction of forms is directed towards the homogenization less of the economic than of the political sphere. This political purpose requires, nonetheless, the industrial production of novelties that are always interchangeable and the immediate, untroubled evocation of affects that are the sign of each individual's identification with the nation. Rather than the auratic remoteness of the modern artwork, the products of kitsch and of nationalism must, by the very logic of their linked economic and political *raisons d'être*, appear *familiar*. Indeed, the sites that they occupy, often to the consternation of both their political and their aesthetic critics, are crucially domestic, those familial spaces in which national desires are safeguarded and reproduced. As Franco Moretti puts it, 'kitsch literally "domesticates" aesthetic experience. It brings it into the home, where most of everyday life takes place.' The correspondence with the strategies of nationalism, which seeks to saturate everyday life, is evident and by no means unrelated to the strategies of religious culture. The sacred heart and votary lamp vie for attention with icons of 1916 in not a few Irish kitchens.[2]

This conjunction of nationalist and religious artefacts as domestic objects raises problems for the purely aesthetic judgement. The rigorous castigation of kitsch relies on the assumption of its impurity or in-authenticity, on its debasement of formerly integral styles into anachronistic stylization, on its tendency to neo-baroque excess. Kitsch is defined as a version of mannerism, sentiment congealed into attitude. Its relation to commodity fetishism in general lies both in its mass-produced standardization of affects and its apparent displacement of authentic social relations. The glossy surfaces and high colour tones, the uncannily familiar yet novel melody, appear to condense feeling into sentiment and to furnish fetishistic subsitutes in place of aesthetic transubstantiations.

For critics of kitsch, Adolf Loos's functionalist horror of ornamentation is typical, not merely in its castigation of mannered stylization or of impossible conjunctions – Grecian ashtrays or Renaissance hatboxes – but more pointedly in his assumption that consumers of kitsch suffer from an outlived primitivism of affect. Kitsch represents a desire for ornament and surface that belongs with savagery and is deeply antagonistic to aesthetic distance.[3] Unlike, say, Marx and Freud, such a theory of fetishism unironically grasps the destruction of aura in the fakeries of kitsch as an effect of the aesthetic underdevelopment of the populace rather than as an inexorable consequence of the social and economic conditions of modernity. Not underdevelopment, but commodity fetishism, which itself dissolves aura into availability and particularity into an advertising slogan, is the fundamental condition which frames the circulation of kitsch. As Adorno remarks, writing of 'commodity music', in the refrain 'Especially for you' the swindle 'is so transparent that it cynically admits it and transfers the special to realms where it loses all meaning'.[4]

The critique of kitsch mistakes its relation to modernity, as the critique of nationalism so often mistakes the relation of its apparent traditionalisms to modernity. But each critique equally mistakes the nature of their relation to distance, aesthetic or historical. Not the stereotype of the savage, subject to immediate impressions, that lurks in Loos's scorn, but the tourist is the proper figure for the lover of kitsch. Not for nothing is the object that springs to mind so often a souvenir, a green Connemara marble Celtic cross or an ashtray embossed with a harp: kitsch is congealed memory that expresses simultaneously the impossible desire to realize a relation to a culture only available in the form of recreation *and* the failure to transmit the past. Kitsch is the inseparable double of an aesthetic culture which continues to pose as a site of redemption for those who are subject to the economic laws of modernity, even in the spaces of recreation that pretend to emancipate them from labour. It is popular culture's indecorous revenge on aesthetic illusion.

As such it is no less a vehicle for feeling, even if, as in the case of religious art, what it reveals is in part the impossibility of integrating aesthetic affect with modernity's fragmentations. The baroque intensities of wounding and mannered suffering in religious art and the fascination with ruins and monuments in tourist kitsch signal the at-homeness of such artefacts in the domain of allegory. They point to the impossibility of achieving organic or symbolic integration of a life, or of a life with art, or of religion into the texture of daily life, precisely in their very insistence within the domestic space. In the very gestures it makes towards transcendence, kitsch preserves the melancholy recognition of the insuperable disjunction between desire and its objects. As Adorno puts it, 'The positive element of kitsch lies in the fact that it sets free for a moment the glimmering realization that you have wasted your life.'[5]

But suppose we amend that comment slightly, to read, 'it sets free for a moment the glimmering realization that your life has been wasted'? This rewriting brings us closer to what is at stake in the resistance of kitsch to aesthetic judgement, to its parodic relation to the redemptive illusions of high culture, and, more importantly, to the significance of kitsch within migrant or colonized cultures. Nowhere are the deracinating and alienating effects of capitalism felt more powerfully than in communities whose histories are determined by domination, displacement and immigration, for whom ruins are the entirely just and not merely figurative indices of living dislocation. And nowhere is kitsch, from the family snapshot to the religious or national icon, more crucial to the articulation of the simultaneous desire for, and impossibility of restoring and maintaining, connection. Kitsch becomes, in such spheres, the congealed memory of traumas too intimate and too profound to be lived over without stylization and attitude. In the migrant community especially, kitsch is subject already to the conditions of inauthenticity that trouble cultural nationalist icons and becomes doubly allegorical of an irredeemable dislocation. The detached fragment that is literally transported is less a memory than the representative of processes of memory which have virtually become unsustainable. It is at once the metonym of transfer and its effects and a sign of the migrant's ambivalent relation to the new and dominant culture. Verbal, musical or visual, the icon stands as a refusal of incorporation that simultaneously challenges a rejection that is in any case inevitable. Is it not the experience of virtually every migrant community to be articulated around icons that are despised by the culture from which we come as no longer authentic (as if its own icons ever were!) and by that to which we come as vulgar, sentimental, gaudy – as signs of underdevelopment and inadequate assimilation? Hence, doubtless, the importance and the recurrence of the feeling of shame in relation to such icons on the part of the assimilating migrant of any generation. The emergence of aesthetic judgement, if only as a regulative standard, has always been instrumental in the formation of citizens.

Yet migrant kitsch and the icons of the dominated are marked by a paradoxical discretion, by what they omit to say as a function of their allegorical mode and of their double obligation. Their allegorical function is to gesture towards a trauma which will not and cannot be fully acknowledged. Will not, by either the culture from which or the culture to which the migrant migrates. For the *emigrant* is the living index of the failure of postcolonial states and is accordingly consigned as rapidly as possible to political oblivion and cultural contempt. The *immigrant*, meanwhile, must be seen in the so-called economic good times, not as the return of imperialism's bad conscience, charged with as much resentment as ambition, but as one seeking the betterment offered by a culturally and economically more dynamic society. S/he must be seen in bad times like the present as a parasite seeking to feed off the vitality of the state s/he undermines, rather than as one more actor in the same global circulations of capital and labour as are transforming social relations with renewed and vicious intensity in every sector and in every region of the world.

In turn, the trauma cannot be fully acknowledged, any more than it can be forgotten, by the migrant or the dominated, for the disavowal of that trauma has the effect of transforming a collective disaster into an individual or familial affair. In the reconstruction of both community and domestic life, the icon functions to contain memory: it at once serves to preserve cultural continuities in face of their disruption and to localize, as it were, the potentially paralyzing effects of trauma and anomie. Take, for example, the strangely moving image above the bar of the Irish Cultural Center in San Francisco, a building in which kitsch thrives at every level, from the architecture to the music.

Irish Cultural Center, San Francisco, 1995. Photo by Ed Kashi

The image, part of a set of black-and-white panels including a round tower and a map of Ireland, appears to represent an emigrant ship. Yet the millions of emigrants who left, and the thousands who died of fever and hunger in the 'coffin ships', are represented only in the couple who occupy a deck that resembles a promenade and whose gaze appears to linger backwards on the homeland, or, possibly, forwards to the land promised to them by the tourist board. Tourists returning or emigrants leaving, a peculiar sense of dislocation hovers in the midst of the nostalgic glow, while, in the bottom right-hand corner, a lone old man stares out from a promontory. There is no evident connection and it is impossible to tell whether he represents the next emigrant or a figure for the reduced but persistent peasant society from which, supposedly, the emigrants fled. In such an icon, the unspeakable trauma of the Great Hunger and of massive emigration over the next century is at once preserved and suppressed.

Yet even the most traumatic memory is never forgotten. If kitsch preserves, in its congealed and privatized, mostly portable forms, the memories of a community that cannot quite be a people, does it not also represent a repertoire which can, in given political circumstances, be redeployed for collective ends? In such cases, the political possibilities derive precisely from the availability of the icon, its constant circulation prior to any politicizing retrieval, and its accumulation in that circulation of individual meanings and attachments, ranging from a shared sense of affection to a shamed sense of stigmatization. In the contradictory range of feelings which attach to it, often simultaneously, lies the secret of the sudden mobility to which the icon can attain in spite of its debasement and devaluation as mere kitsch. One such instance would be the figure of Mother Ireland, a figure generally decried by the agents of modernity as a residue of atavistic Victorian celticism, yet whose recirculation in the recent decades of the Troubles has transformed her into a site of profound contestations over the meaning and definition of women's struggles and their relation to republicanism and cultural nationalism. As the superb documentary by the Derry Film Collective, *Mother Ireland*, indicates, it is precisely the contradictoriness of the affects that attach to such icons that permits their transformation from scleroticized to dynamic cultural forms, forms available for contestation and revision. Something similar has been the case with the refiguration of cultural icons like La Malinche and La Virgen de Guadalupe by Chicana artists and writers like Yolanda M. Lopez, Ester Hernandez or Cherrie Moraga.[6]

It is important to emphasize this fact that the sources of the icons thus refigured are so often exactly those which have been recirculated, commodified, apparently exhausted in the turns of reproduction and circulation. There is nothing atavistic or regressive in the cultural politics which reappropriates icons long denigrated as vulgar kitsch. On the contrary, what such art often maps is the problematic and often ironic interface between the economic and therefore cultural and political force of modernity and the survival of the alternative spaces of the non-modern. Their political meaning lies in the jarring juxtaposition of motifs that are not so much traditional as attenuated by familiarity with motifs derived from the conditions of struggle against postmodern state violence. Some of Gerry Kelly's most powerful murals in West Belfast derive their iconography not from ancient celtic manuscripts but from Jim Fitzpatrick's post-Marvel celtic comic, *The Book of Conquests*. As he has

Peter John Caraher at home. Photo by Mike Abrahams/Network

remarked, this involved a quite conscious transfer in the art he had begun painting on handkerchiefs while in the H-Blocks, a move from the permitted kitsch of Ireland's official religious and commodity cultures to the stylization of celtic mythology:

> Prison was supposed to be a breaker's yard for republicans. You were stripped of your dignity, your clothes, anything that showed your identity. You were allowed to paint hankies of the Pope, the Virgin Mary, Mickey Mouse and things like that. They censored everything. [After reading Fitzpatrick] Rather than do the Mickey Mouse things, I decided to paint Celtic mythology.[7]

Kelly's repertoire, not unlike that of contemporary Chicano muralists, is drawn from numerous sources, ranging from Sandinista murals to newspaper cartoons. At the same time, the mural as a form exists in *situ* and often gains its exact meanings from its relation not only to a very definite community but also to the forces of state power against which the mural speaks in its very vulnerability and relative poverty of material resources. In this sense, it enacts an ironic reversal of the ways in which the state's counter-insurgency apparatuses have tried to produce a simulacrum of the non-modern 'knowable community', where so much knowledge passes by intimate channels, in the form of computerized databanks that can access the name of your neighbour's dog or listening devices that can eavesdrop on every living-room or street-corner conversation.

From one perspective, the effects of work like Kelly's, or of Mission district muralists in San Francisco, are not remote from those of Mexican American artist Ruben Ortiz Torres's video work *Para Leer Macho Mouse* (1993), with its extravagant and ironic deployment of Disney and commodified Mexicanisms. Nor are they far in spirit from his adapted baseball caps, in which a radical juxtaposition of the all-American headgear with the homeboy's appropriation of that dominant icon is spelt out in the adaptations of the caps' letterings. These are supposed to signal legitimate affiliations, but instead come to bear memories of expropriation, stigma and resistance: 1492, Mestizo, Aztlan. Nor are such murals far from the work of Northern Irish artist John Kindness's double-edged play with the outrageous convergence of the kitsch of both dominant and unofficial cultures: the Ninja harp or the Grecian cab door. Kindness's work plays, in such images, on the horror with which Loos observed Grecian ashtrays or Gothic chandeliers in late nineteenth-century Vienna; in doing so, he liberates from aesthetic judgements much the same wit and mobility which allows subordinated cultures to rediscover in 'kitsch' a rich repertoire for resistance.

These artworks resume some of the functions and processes of the recovery of kitsch from street elements, yet, doing so within the gallery-space, effectively re-aestheticize a mode of work that derives its very significance from its breach of the separation between public and recreationary space. Where Ortiz Torres's and Kindness's work tends to terminate in the gallery or other spaces for quasi-private consumption, its function is properly and critically to enter and disturb aesthetic expectations within a distinct cultural space, and in turn to stimulate a reperception of the resources of popular kitsch or of quotidian artefacts. It remains a largely ironic citation of those forms, aimed at a reflective rather than situated engagement with the politics of culture.[8]

'Scraping the Surface' 1990, by John Kindness

'Ninja Turtle Harp' 1991, by John Kindness

The distinguishing aesthetic characteristic of a politicized mural art is its virtual uncitability: its meaning and function are inseparable from the space of its production and consumption, from the various vistas of approach to it, from its relation to a community and communal memories, and from its embeddedness in quite specific projects. The work of Gerry Kelly, and other more or less anonymous/collective muralists, operates within a highly politicized public space where the interface between a commodified post-modernity and non-modern resistance grounds the signification of multiple layers of cultural elements. It reconstitutes public space, not as the now largely corporatized site of manufactured consent, but as the locus of antag-onisms between incommensurable social imaginaries. In this space, as we have already seen in the chapter 'True Stories', the distinction between the public sphere as the site of political discussion and negotiation and the pri-vate or domestic sphere collapses, insofar as the latter becomes the site of the reproduction and dissemination of alternative political narrative. The insistent juxtaposition of different temporalities and their redisposition as contemporaneous elements in a provisional unity signals at once a radically alternative aesthetic mode and another conception of public space. The ironic distance that subtends equally the good subject of civil society and the proper relation to the aesthetic object is not at play here: the mural operates not as a means to ironize the inadequacy of atrophied aesthetic modes by juxtaposing them with contemporary commodity forms, for example, but as a way to emphasize the discrete but unhistoricized conti-nuities of cultural resistance.

Mural by Gerry Kelly commemorating eight IRA volunteers killed during an ambush of Loughal Barracks, Belfast, 1988. Photo by Laurie Sparham/Network

Unhistoricized because, to recur to Benjamin's terms, the alternative memories of the past are constituted always in relation to the relentless forward movement of developmental historicism that constitutes the alternative as *passé*. Thus, when Gerry Kelly juxtaposes the images of IRA volunteers ambushed at Lough Gall with a stylized Irish landscape retrieved from Jim Fitzpatrick, the appeal is not to nostalgia for an unbroken spirit of Irish identity but to the fragmentary tableau that constitutes the memory of constant efforts to realize other ways of living in the face of unrelenting domination. Nor is it a utopian imagination withdrawn from actual social relations: the Irish landscape is painted on a gable end that slips in a long perspective along the bleak façade of terraced houses in a new estate, from which long rows of tricolour bunting reach out to the other side of the street. The mural in its location not only articulates its own elements in juxtaposition but articulates with its site as a further element in a yet larger tableau. The photographic image reproduced here fortuitously extends that tableau while at the same time troubling its stasis: the figure of the young girl crossing the street between the camera and the mural, tripping along in adult shoes, ironizes any desire to fix the rhythms of reception of the scene. Her gaze, obliquely continuing those of the dead volunteers, stares down the fixative desire of the archivist to freeze the tableau in time.

The historicist desire to put subaltern memory in its place, to fix its proper moment in historical time, exceeds its accomplishment. In another mural Kelly, this time in collaboration with Ruben Ortiz Torres, juxtaposes the figures of James Connolly, the national Marxist republican executed in 1916, and Emilio Zapata, the leader of rural indigenous movements in the Mexican revolution of 1910, with figures of a contemporary IRA volunteer and a Zapatista guerrilla. Such an image notoriously outrages historicist sense and liberal political-aesthetic judgement. It appears to suggest an at once transhistorical and transnational identity between moments and movements and, in doing so, to repudiate the state's criminalization project. That the latter effect is part and parcel of the significance of such works is hardly deniable; any assumption that the effect betrays the primitive immediacy of unreflective historical conscious-ness is one based on ideological disavowal. What is often stigmatized as iden-tity politics – and usually then as hostage to myth – might better be termed historical politics. Connolly signifies here not as an archetypal martyr in Republican hagiography, nor merely as an icon of an unchanging Republican ideology, but as an index of the historical formation of contemporary condi-tions. Connolly's work was directed against both colonial and capitalist domi-nation in Ireland; his early successes in organizing in both northern and southern Ireland along non-sectarian class lines were a major factor in the intensification and eventual institutionalization of Protestant supremacy in Northern Ireland by unionist élites. His invocation here signifies at once an invocation of non-sectarian socialism and an analysis of the conditions of con-tinuing segregation, social injustice and political marginalization out of which the present struggle has emerged as one which must continue to engage colo-nial capitalism even beyond the fight for a united Ireland. By the same token, his contemporary, Zapata, is invoked in Mexico precisely at the moment when the pressures of global capitalism led the Mexican government to abandon the constitutional protections for traditional indigenous landholdings that the rev-olutionary movements he led had inscribed in the constitution.[9]

In common between Connolly and Zapata is that their continuing rele-vance in the present is a function of the violent efforts of the state to repress and to occlude their significance. Within republican or indigenous commun-ities, their survival constitutes an alternative to the inroads of capitalist colo-nial developments and a genealogy of the conditions of the present which make alternatives crucial. Again, the forms of domination and their historical meaning are constituted along the lines of their encounter with groups whose very survival, whose very 'memory banks', would have to be erased in order for those forms to seem self-evident. Simultaneously, there appear along this line different modes of subjectivity than those of the liberal political subject of modernity. The term subjectivity implies in itself a concept quite at odds with the autonomous and disinterested subject-as-spectator of liberal civil society. The formation of subjectivities entails rather the emergence, in spaces constitutively barred from access to civil society, of social agents the condition of whose survival lies in perpetual differentiation from the norms of dominant society and whose cultural practices are persistently recalcitrant to state pro-jects. I insist on the plural here, since the emergence of such subjectivities is not the consequence of individual dissonance or of falterings in subject for-mation but is at one, as a process, with the differential constitution of the state itself. Subjectivity, in this sense, is not an individual affair but an effect of the necessary marginalization or erasure of constitutively inassimilable social groups from citizenship in the nation-state. The concept of subjectivity accordingly entails a drive beyond incorporation into a reformed state and towards a total transformation of the terms of sociality itself.[10]

The confrontation of differentiated cultures and their subjectivities with the state is a global phenomenon intensified by the postcolonial conditions in which the nation-state has become the internationally canonical political institution.[11] This phenomenon does much to explain the complex and migrant dialectic between local sites and global processes with which this chapter, and, indeed, this book, have been much concerned. Each distinct state is differentiated out of unique and particular local circumstances which are at once preserved and transformed in this process. But the virtual universality of the state form, in its ubiquitous imposition as in its claims to historical pre-eminence, produces an effect of structural identity among quite distinct sites of resistance. Struggles against the state are simultaneously struggles against the universal extension of transnational capital through the medium of the state of which Fanon presciently warned in *The Wretched of the Earth*. For this reason, the conditions of struggle require at one and the same time the recognition of structurally similar relations and the insistence on cultural differentiation as the very form of the survival of alternatives to global homogenization. That differentiation is no less the form in which resistance is constantly cast. In that case, what passes for kitsch in the light of aesthetic judgement is recovered as the emblem of cultures that have been cast from futurity by the state, as commodities are thrown out of circulation, only to discover in their wasted particulars the elements of another living.

EPILOGUE
'Living in America':
Politics and Emigrations

'Working with the black man, Dominican and Greek . . .
Mammy dear, we're all mad over here,
Livin' in America.'
(Lyrics from Black 47, 'Livin' in America')

In the United States of late, the notion of 'diaspora' has become more and more frequently invoked by ethnic groups to describe the global dispersion of their populations. The word derives of course from the Greek word for the scattering of the Jews after the destruction of the temple by the Romans in the first century AD. But the term *diaspora* has lately been extended to cover the experiences not only of African Americans, North, South and Caribbean, but also of Asian Americans, most particularly the Chinese in their connections to Chinese cultures throughout the world, and South Asians living in the Americas, Europe, the Caribbean and Africa. There is also an Arab diaspora, particularly the Palestinian version which quite deliberately inverts the notion of the Jewish diaspora by highlighting how the establishment of a Jewish homeland meant the displacement of the Palestinian population in turn. Of late, talk about the Irish diaspora has proliferated: we are, after all, a population scattered by dispossession, transportation, exile and emigration throughout the world, though mostly throughout the 'English-speaking world' of the formerly British settler colonies.

The term is powerfully affective. For the Jews, it was and continues to be a term which encapsulates not simply scattering, but the survival of a culture, a religion and an ethos through the many and various forms and disguises which exile historically demanded. The survival of the culture principally turned on two things: the 'book' (or Talmud) and the hope of an eventual return to the promised land, though the idea of return was often allegorical rather than actual.

As the notion of diaspora has been taken up by other communities here in the USA, the emphasis has mostly been on the cultural meaning rather than the idea of return. This has been especially true of the African adoptions of the term: there are few enough African Americans now for whom the notion of a return to the homeland is a powerful or even viable one. But in so far as diaspora refers to the survival of cultural forms and values through all the vicissitudes of exile, it has a vital emotional and, more importantly, political significance. The long tradition of African American scholarship, which has only recently begun to gain some of the respect it deserves, has constantly sought to demonstrate how African cultural and religious practices, languages and social forms survived, even if in disguised or hybridized ways, throughout slavery and the dispersal and mixing of African peoples in the 'New World'. Though often caricatured in mainstream publications, the understanding of the continuity as well as the breaking and destruction of African cultures has been an invaluable means to affirming black political identity in a racist society.

Yet I hesitate to welcome the extension of the term to the Irish community here. It is not just that conditions for Irish Americans are entirely different than those for other ethnic groups. Though they are: for all the long struggle of Irish immigrants to gain acceptance in the United States against deep religious and racial prejudice, Irish Americans are now a fully integrated element of white and mainstream American society. Irish 'illegals', immigrants without the green card, are rarely picked up in random sweeps of the Mission District of San Francisco or South Central Los Angeles, unlike their Latin American and even Chicano counterparts, many of whom turn out to be citizens after all. Return is no longer a powerful emotional idea for Irish Americans, except in the mostly sentimental and fetishizing desire to establish their genealogy in the old country. That desire has been augmented recently by the successes of a liberal multiculturalism that has left many white Americans, whose roots are by now twisted and entangled in the soil of several European lands, seeking the cultural distinctiveness that they have learnt to see as the 'privilege' of ethnic minorities.

It is this very sentimental and thoroughly depoliticized desire that threatens to be confirmed in the notion of an Irish diaspora. Writing in *The Irish Reporter*, the Irish broad left quarterly, Mary Corcoran quoted one American Irish immigrant leader as saying that:

> There is an Irish nation, but it is a diaspora. We are like the Jews. Ireland is a home base – like Israel, the promised land. We cannot all live on one small island, we have too much to offer the world.[1]

The invocation of an 'Irish diaspora' has the effect of naturalizing the continuing massive outflow of skilled and unskilled labour from Ireland, as if there were some given population level for the island that we have already exceeded. But, as we know, demographic projections from the moment of independence would have estimated the probable population of the Republic for 1990 as around fourteen rather than four million. Only the constant haemorrhage of emigration has kept the population so low and, as Declan Kiberd and others suggested in the same issue of the *Reporter*, so apparently conservative.[2]

In the often sentimental memorialization of the Famine and of the continuing mass emigration that followed it, little mention has, till recently, been made of the massive restructuring of Irish society that followed it. Yet of the millions who left in the second half of the nineteenth century and since, the vast majority were the landless and largely disenfranchised working classes. Their departure consolidated the political and economic power of the large and middling farmers who have been described as the 'nation-building class'. And of course the nation-state they built, for numerous reasons, largely conformed to their interests and ideology: conservative, principally agricultural and dominated by the most conservative kind of Catholicism imaginable. The classes among which opposition to such a polity thrived, and who throughout the War of Independence stood for quite radical transformation of the society, created soviets and maintained if not an anti-clerical at least an anti-episcopal stance, were decimated by emigration.

The term *emigration* has accordingly its own resonances both in Ireland and abroad, resonances not simply echoing from ballads like 'Spancil Hill', 'The Leaving of Liverpool' or 'Carrickfergus', but with both folk and historical recollections of famine, of eviction, of dispossession and of economic depression and failure. The term itself bears for us the reminder of the political and economic legacies of colonialism and, particularly where Irish emigrants meet those from other nations, the shock of recognition of our alignment with the postcolonial world that so many would have us forget. Emigration is not the spontaneous overflow of surplus population from a land without contraception, but part of a pattern of movements of labour linked to systemic underdevelopment as surely as transnational capital flows are linked to the global disequilibria of wealth, exploitation and consumption. To give but one striking instance, it is with the Philippines that Ireland is paired as the world's greatest exporters of female nursing and domestic service workers.

Emigration is a slow and individualized national trauma, often sentimentalized and dressed up by the very cultural forms, most importantly music, that have helped the emigrant to survive. Its very slowness and the fact that it is apprehended by individuals and families in ways that statistics fail to touch, prevent that trauma from being sufficiently engaged at the political level. We grow up anticipating departure in ways that deeply affect the culture. But that experience is not unique to Ireland: multicultural America is built on immigration from countries marked by imperial wars and conquests, anti-colonial and decolonizing struggles, economic exploitation and the massive migration of peoples. The streets and public schools of Los Angeles, San Francisco and New York accommodate the children of workers from the Philippines, Mexico, Korea, Laos, Vietnam, Cambodia, El Salvador, Puerto Rico, Haiti, as well as the many who claim some Irish heritage.

Where the invocation of 'diaspora' tends to emphasize, and even to celebrate, the mostly *cultural* by-products of nearly two centuries of Irish migrations, that of emigration keeps in mind both the economic and political reasons for our leaving and helps to affirm the vital relation between our historical experience and that of other decolonizing societies. Constantly to recall this is the political work of the emigrant communities. One aspect of the accidental political effects of emigration is said to be that many from the Republic become aware for the first time of the issues underlying the Northern conflict simply because they for the first time meet people from Belfast or Derry. But there is also the effect of English racism on Irish people coming to Birmingham or London that helps them understand the perspective of British blacks, or the encounter in San Francisco with Chicanos and Latinos that helps us situate our experience in terms of the larger global history of the New World Order.

In 1847, hundreds of Irish soldiers in the Anglo-American army fighting against Mexico deserted to form the San Patricio Corps, identifying with the Mexican people. Mostly Irish-speaking, they had undergone the racism of their Anglo officers and watched the burning of Catholic churches and the rape and slaughter of Mexicans. Their understanding of the links between English domination of Ireland and Yankee domination of Mexico was immediate. Many died in the war and many were executed by the US for desertion, but the descendants of the survivors, Spanish-speaking Mexicans, still meet to commemorate the brigade in Mexico City. In 1993, Luis Camnitzer, an Argentinian Jewish artist based in the US, held an exhibition in Mexico City commemorating the San Patricios. These intersections between Irish and Latin-American experiences continue, though they are less well known than the stories of Irish presidents and film stars. Catriona Ruane has written eloquently of how her own experiences in Nicaragua prepared her to understand the situation in Belfast on her return to Ireland.[3] These are not the 'typical' experiences of the Irish diaspora in popular media and myth, but they are crucial examples of the ways in which experiences in emigration can be politicizing in ways that affect not only our understanding of 'abroad' but also what we want to bring back home. These are ways in which we can make a new sense of our dispersion, historically and in the present. But, as the current conservative resistance to a campaign led by the Labour Party in Ireland to grant an emigrant vote indicates, we still need to find collective ways to bring our experience home and make it count.

But we also need to find ways to make it active here in the United States. The longer history of the Irish-American experience has tended to be more about the separation of the Irish immigrants from the people of colour here, at least insofar as it has been a matter of official historical record. That history is in some senses the familiar one of dividing and ruling. The Cromwellian depopulation of Ireland in the seventeenth century sent thousands of Irish to the Caribbean as slaves and indentured servants alongside Africans, giving rise to the 'redshanks' of the West Indies. Records of plantation owners show the anxieties created among slaveowners by the apparent solidarity between

Irish and black slaves. By the mid-nineteenth century, a different era of Irish immigration resulted at first in those savage mainstream caricatures of both the Irish and the black as equivalently degenerate races that L. P. Curtis has so well documented. For Anglo-Saxons, 'Celt' and 'Negro' were a comparable threat to their society.

But things changed with the increasing political and labour power of the Irish, which Joseph Lee suggested came about through a combination of their superior competence in English over other European groups and the practice in political mass organization that they brought with them from the many anti-colonial struggles in Ireland.[4] Rather than the shared experience of discrimination leading to solidarity with black or Chinese workers, the Irish adhered to the new racial category of 'whiteness', by and large becoming, through the police force, the labour unions and the city political machines, the agents of the dominant racial formation of the United States.[5] Given such a history, it is surely impossible now for Irish Americans to evoke the memory of their experience of discrimination as some kind of ethical hedge against their access to what is still the privilege of whiteness. Of course one hears, all too frequently, the retort in debates around affirmative action or ethnic relations that 'we had to struggle too', and this simplified history of the Irish struggle for integration into dominant American culture has given shape in a more scholarly version to the formulations of Nathan Glazer and Daniel Moynihan. For them, exactly those trials of European, and especially Irish, immigrants provide the ideal model for American narratives of successful immigration and assimilation. This makes it all the more important for us to open up the other histories that are less often invoked, difficult as that may be.

The project is not to comfort Irish Americans for now occupying the ethically unenviable position of being identified as white, whether by reminding them of their own history of oppression in this country or by cultivating a re-ethnicizing obsession with roots. The project is rather to begin to trace alternative histories, histories which may not spell success in terms of the dominant paradigm, and may even, like the San Patricios, spell a certain kind of failure. Alongside the well-documented history of the gradual assimilation of Irish immigrants into American culture, there must be many, less well-documented memories of other decisions and other affiliations which Irish labourers and peasants made on the basis of their own experiences of racism and colonialism. We need to retrieve these stories, not so that they can become another dominant history, displacing the former, but so that they can form a repertoire for what I would call the history of possibilities, thinking, once again, of the ways in which even the defeated struggles and gestures of the oppressed remain in memory to re-emerge as the impulse to new forms of solidarity. These stories serve to remind us that the history of the integration of Ireland and the Irish into Western modernity is not only not the only story but also not the only possibility. Our history is full of reasons to seek out both international and inter-ethnic connections, because of what we know and because of what we could know better of ourselves and of others. And because the struggle against injustice is not ended just by our own becoming 'legal'.

I write as an Irish citizen living in America and write therefore with a double consciousness and a dual interest. The recent intensification of racialized politics in the United States, by which recent Irish immigrants, whether documented or undocumented, are directly and acutely addressed, demands our response. This is a moment in which Irish migrants must either choose solidarity with people of colour or once more hide under the veil of our whiteness. But that choice has repercussions in Ireland and for Irish political directions also. Perhaps more than for any generation of emigrants, the current generation can be alert to the geopolitical meaning of mass emigration. Though many of us are professionals, able easily to integrate into the middle classes of our host societies, the vast majority of emigrants continue to be working class, displaced by the conditions of postcolonial dependency or continuing colonial occupation. Many of even those who have been privileged and qualified by class and education come away politically and culturally disaffected from the longstanding conservatism of the official Irish nation, leaving Ireland as much in disgust as by necessity. In addition, almost thirty years of cultural as well as armed anti-colonial struggle in the North of Ireland, a struggle which, more fully than at any previous moment in Irish republicanism, has affirmed its links with other insurgencies globally and had profound effects on our sense of possible affiliation. More than ever, this is a moment in which it is possible for Irish emigrants both to identify with and learn from the issues of Third World and minority peoples and to direct some of the lessons learnt homewards. As the Irish élites rush towards integration into the new, racialized 'Fortress Europe', and the incidence of racist violence against our own immigrant and minority communities climbs, we emigrants need to reinvoke our colonized past. We must be active, not only in an America which continues to play out the gambits of colonialism internally and externally, but also in Ireland, bringing back home the knowledge that integration with the dominant order has never been the only or the most liberating possibility.

As I write now months after the ratification of the Peace Accord, these considerations seem all the more urgent. I have in mind not just the insistence of triumphalist and Klan-like sectarianism nor the resumption of political violence, though these will certainly legitimate the maintenance of the British state's enormous security apparatus. Yet more important are the deep structural inadequacies of the peace process itself. The probable failure of this latest in a series of reconciliatory initiatives will lie less in the work of extremists than in the very conditions established from the outset for the process: that the legitimacy of neither the British nor the Irish state could be in question. This condition has amounted to the mutual disavowal of the actual agency of both states in the conflict, of their maintenance of power through an arbitrary monopoly on the use of repressive force, of, in short, the colonial constitution of contemporary Ireland. Instead, each state has retained, in different ways, the convenient fantasy role of being arbiters, disinterested spectators of a process that is 'local' in its causes and in its effects.

In consequence, the political resolution that has been proposed with such acclaim preserves the colonial relations that structure Ireland's economic, political and cultural formations. It seems clear that the accord was reached in large part by the promise of international investment, specifically from the USA, and that it facilitates further integration into the European Community's regional system. The strategy is familiar from the post-war era: the integration of sites of decolonization into the capitalist world order has generally taken place through economic rationalization and development, which have been increasingly held, despite all the evidence, to lead in turn to the political and cultural 'modernization' of civil society. More often than not, it has led instead to the increased exploitation of working people, environmental destruction and the repression of alternative movements globally through the combined work of neo-colonial states and transnational corporations.

What, then, will be the cost of this peace process that has been made hostage to the old state forms and to accelerated transnational investment and extraction? The reconstruction of Ireland, unified or not, will be meaningless if paid for by the exploitation of low-paid Irish workers: if global patterns are realized, not only will those workers' rights be difficult to protect, due to the absence of strong, non-sectarian labour organizations in the North, but the spaces available for labour organizing will be relentlessly assaulted and diminished, north and south of the border. Already, cycles of employment and unemployment to which the Republic has been subject have not helped to reduce the rates of emigration and there seems little likelihood that this will change in an Ireland at peace. Failing an international economic slump, emigration will not cease to be a principal means of regulating civil dissent.

At the very start of the negotiations, Bernadette Devlin McAliskey raised the question that remains most pertinent: what, under the conditions set by the peace process, will become of the social movements and the popular democracy that have been at the core of alternative visions of what a united Ireland might be?[6] These, and the related flourishing of alternative cultural organizations and practices over the last twenty years or so, are entirely out of kilter with the economic regionalism of Europe, for which cultural difference is merely a commodifiable ornament laid over the homogenizing processes of capitalist rationalization. Sustained as they have been by a common rejection of the state, what can be the space for alternative cultural forms in a peace that is to be regulated everywhere by state institutions?

McAliskey's reflections remind us that the goal of unification is only one element in a project that is profoundly one of decolonization rather than formal independence. The unity of Ireland in itself is of less value than the transformation of Ireland. This is the project that republicanism shares with labour movements, with radical feminism and with environmental activists, and it is a project that involves the radical rethinking of all our political imaginaries.

Rethinking our political ends and strategies will draw on the rich repertoire of alternative social practices in Ireland as well as the dehierarchization of traditional assumptions and practices. But it will need to draw no less on the practices of decolonization and the struggles against the New World Order that continue all over the map, among minority communities in the industrial world as in the postcolonial nation-states. These form a network of alternative practices from which we can learn as much by our differences as by our identifications.

In this project of transformation, Irish emigrants can play a specific role beyond that of interpreting the Troubles to curious citizens abroad. Disenfranchised as we may be in relation to the Irish state, we are not necessarily disenfranchised in relation to transformative social movements in Ireland. At a pragmatic level, we are constantly in contact in our daily lives with other migrant workers and activists, with minority activists and intellectuals, and with other postcolonial subjects, not to mention our contacts with Irish people from very different communities. The state of emigration is one that obliges rethinking as well as mobility, involving adaptation to a different set of cultures and a constantly changing perspective on Irish culture itself. In this respect, we can bring to Irish debates an engagement with grasping Irish concerns within an international context of struggles for radical change, ranging from a practical grasp of the social and ecological effects of the new technological and bio-technological industries to an analytical understanding of social movements that may be inspired by encounters with local and migrant intellectuals and activists. This commitment is, of course, inseparable from our commitment to transformation within our states of residence. Experienced in terms of a new politics, living away becomes less an experience of amputation and melancholy than a shared means to living otherwise.

NOTES

Introduction

1. Walter Benjamin, 'Theses on the Philosophy of History' in *Illuminations*, trans. Harry Zohn (New York: Schocken, 1969), pp. 253–64; epigraph, p. 257.

2. For a more extended elaboration of the concept of the 'non-modern', see the Introduction to Lisa Lowe and David Lloyd, (eds.), *The Politics of Culture in the Shadow of Capital* (Durham, NC: Duke University Press, 1997).

3. '*What Ish My Nation?*': *Themes in Irish History, 1550–1850*, ed. Thomas Bartlett et al. (Dublin: Gill and Macmillan, 1988), pp. 44–59.

4. Ibid., p. 46.

5. Ibid., p. 47.

6. Ibid., p. 47.

7. Ibid., p. 47.

8. On 'rational abstraction' see Karl Marx, *A Contribution to the Critique of Political Economy*, ed. Maurice Dobb, trans. S. W. Ryazanskaya (Moscow: Progress Publishers, 1970), pp. 205–13.

9. Ian Lustick, *Unsettled States, Disputed Lands: Britain and Ireland, France and Algeria, Israel and the West Bank–Gaza* (Ithaca, N.Y.: Cornell University Press, 1993).

10. On the growing significance of the notion of 'national character' in Ireland, see Seamus Deane, *Strange Country: Modernity and Nationhood in Irish Writing since 1790* (Oxford: Oxford University Press, 1997).

11. Liam Kennedy, 'Post-Colonial Society or Post-Colonial Pretensions?,' in *Colonialism, Religion and Nationalism in Ireland* (Belfast: Queen's University Institute for Irish Studies, 1996), pp. 167–81. In opening the essay, Kennedy ventures a little sarcasm at the expense of Parnell and Pearse, both of whom compared conditions in Ireland to those of slaves in the United States. He seems blithely unaware that this comment had previously been made by Gustave de Beaumont, friend of de Tocqueville and well-respected travel writer, and by no less a figure than Frederick Douglass, who might have had reason to know. One could multiply the list of US and other foreign visitors who made similar comparisons irrespective of their relation to nationalism.

12. Ibid., p. 169.

13. Ibid., p. 169.

14. *Pace* Liam Kennedy, there have been several quite extended analyses of Ireland as a nation that has suffered from, in Frank Gunder Andre's term, 'capitalist underdevelopment'. The most notable of these is to be found in Raymond Crotty's all too neglected *Ireland in Crisis: A Study in Capitalist Colonial Underdevelopment* (Dingle: Brandon Books, 1986), chapters 5 and 6. For direct comparison with Latin America, see Colm Regan, 'Latin American Dependency Theory and its Relevance to Ireland' in *The Crane Bag* 6, no. 2 (1982), pp. 15–20. Carol Coulter's *Ireland: between the First and the Third Worlds* (Dublin: Attic Press LIP Pamphlet, 1990) engages in a more political analysis of Ireland's resemblances to Latin America.

15.   Liam Kennedy, 'Post-Colonial Society or Post-Colonial Pretensions', p. 170.

16.   On the current ratio of investment to profit outflow in Ireland, see Denis O'Hearn, 'The Celtic Tiger: The Role of the Multi-nationals' in Jim MacLaughlin and Ethel Crowley, *Under the Belly of the Tiger: Class, Race, Identity and Culture in the Global Ireland* (Dublin: Irish Reporter Publications, 1997), pp. 21–34. For Ireland's agricultural 'undevelopment' in relation to colonial capitalism, see again Crotty, *Ireland in Crisis*, esp. chapter 4.

17.   For a discussion of work of this kind on imperialism by the Marxist Lenin and the liberal J.A. Hobson, see Wolfgang J. Mommsen, *Theories of Imperialism*, trans. P.S. Falla (New York: Random House, 1980), pp. 47–53 and 11–19 respectively.

18.   See Kerby Miller, *Emigrants and Exiles* (Oxford: Oxford University Press, 1985), p. 569.

19.   The term 'imagined communities' is usually taken from the celebrated book of that title by Benedict Anderson. My usage of that term here is borrowed from Chandra Talpade Mohanty's redefinition of it in 'Cartographies of Struggle: Third World Women and the Politics of Feminism', introduction to Chandra Talpade Mohanty, Ann Russo and Lourdes Torres (eds.), *Third World Women and the Politics of Feminism*, (Bloomington: Indiana University Press, 1991), p. 4.

20.   The performative is a mode of utterance which inaugurates a new state: "Let there be light!", and there was light' being the ultimate instance. Where the divine performative is held to be absolutely inaugural, human utterances derive their power to alter states from an assumed anterior institutional authority: the Church, the state, the university, the discipline: 'I declare you man and wife', or 'I am President'. J.L. Austin discusses the performance in this sense *in How to Do Things With Words* (Cambridge, MA: Harvard University Press, 1962). Yet, at the same time, the power of the institution is only realized in such utterances and in their acceptance by those affected by them. In this respect, the performative is a consensual fiction that organizes a community and its relations of authority. It is no less subject to 'iteration', the performative always being a citation of a prior encoded utterance. Accordingly, we can say that it is only in its iteration that the authority of any institution is affirmed, each time anew, so that in fact the institution depends on its iteration rather than on any actual founding moment. Jacques Derrida analyzes this problematic in "Signature Event Context", in *Margins of Philosophy*, trans. Alan Bass (Chicago: Chicago University Press, 1982), pp. 307–330. This opens the space for the parodic destabilization of the performative as *performance*; or for the skewing of official history in its daily reiterations and popular appropriations. For excellent elaboration of the socially destabilizing effects of performativity, in the areas of gender and colonialism respectively, see Judith Butler, *Gender Trouble: Feminism and the Subversion of Identity* (New York: Routledge, 1990), pp. 145–149, and Homi Bhabha, "DissemiNation", in *Nation and Narration*, ed. Homi Bhabha (New York: Routledge, 1990), pp. 297–300. One special instance of the performative and its destabilizing effects is the declaration of Independence, which constitutes the very people in whose name it claims to speak, while at the same time exposing the arbitrariness of foundation by delegitimating the previously constituted state in power. Though Derrida's *Declarations d'Indépendance*, in *Otobiographies: l'enseignement de Nietsche et la politique du nom propre* (Paris: Editions

de Galilee, 1984), pp. 11–32 addresses the American document, the Irish version of 1916 is itself an interesting variant of the same problematic, which it performs in the very insistence on the provisionality of its authority.

21. I refer here to Edward Said's *Orientalism* (1979), Frantz Fanon's *Black Skin, White Masks* (1952) and *The Wretched of the Earth* (1961), Chinua Achebe's *Things Fall Apart* (1958), or Chandra T. Mohanty's essay, 'Under Western Eyes' (1984). These writings, among some others, have proven to be seminal texts of theoretical work on colonialism. The best anthology of work on colonialism currently is Patrick Williams and Laura Chrisman (eds.), *Colonial Discourse and Post-colonial Theory* (New York: Columbia University Press, 1994).

22. Stuart Hall, 'Gramsci's Relevance for the Study of Race and Ethnicity', *Journal of Communication Inquiry* 10 (Summer 1986), pp. 5-27.

23. On Trevelyan's career as a colonial administrator, see S. B. Cooke, *Imperial Affinities: Nineteenth-Century Analogies and Exchanges Between India and Ireland* (New Delhi: Sage, 1993); and for a recent discussion of Trevelyan's attitudes to the Famine, see Peter Gray, 'Ideology and the Famine' in Cathal Portéir (ed.), *The Great Irish Famine* (Cork: Mercier, 1995), pp. 86–103.

24. For Brigadier Frank Kitson's writings, see his *Low Intensity Operations: Subversion, Insurgency and Peace-Keeping* (London: Faber, 1971) and *Bunch of Five* (London: Faber and Faber, 1977), an account of his involvement in several postwar colonial campaigns, including Kenya, Malaya, Muscat and Oman, and Cyprus. On the general logic of counter-insurgency, also written from the perspective of the military and the state, see Andrew M. Scott, *Insurgency* (Chapel Hill: University of North Carolina Press, 1970). I have discussed the concept and effects of low-intensity warfare as used in counter-insurgency in the chapters 'Regarding Ireland in a Postcolonial Frame' and 'True Stories'.

25. See Gauri Viswenathan, *Masks of Conquest: Literary Study and British Rule in India* (New York: Columbia University Press, 1989) and KumKum Sangari, "Relating Histories: Definitions of Literacy, Literature, Gender in Early Nineteenth Century Calcutta and England", in *Rethinking English: Essays in Literature, Language, History*, ed. Srati Joshi (New Delhi: Trianka, 1991), pp. 32–123, on the question of education; David Arnold, *Police Power and Colonial Rule: Madras, 1859–1947* (Delhi: Oxford University Press, 1986) and Nasser Hussain, *The Jurisprudence of Emergency: Sovereignty and the Rule of Law in British India* (U.C. Berkeley: Ph.D. Dissertation, 1993), for studies of policing and the law.

26. Kevin Barry, 'Critical Notes on Post-colonial Aesthetics', *Irish Studies Review* 14 (Spring 1996), pp. 6-7. His argument here is directed principally at Luke Gibbons, 'Identity without a Centre' in *Transformations in Irish Culture: Allegory, History and Irish Nationalism* (Cork: Cork University Press, 1996), pp. 134–148 and at my own essay, 'Violence and the Constitution of the Novel', *Anomalous States: Irish Writing and the Postcolonial Moment* (Dublin: Lilliput and Durham, NC: Duke University Press, 1993), pp. 125–62.

27. See Dipesh Chakrabarty, *Rethinking Working-Class History, Bengal 1890–1940* (Princeton, NJ: Princeton University Press, 1989); Partha Chatterjee, *Nationalist Thought and the Colonial World: A Derivative Discourse?* (London: Zed Books, 1986); Kum Kum Sangari and Sudesh Vaid, *Recasting Women: Essays in Indian Colonial History* (Delhi: Kali for Women, 1989); Reynaldo Ileto, *Pasyon and Revolution: Popular Movements in the Philippines, 1840–1910* (Manila: Ateneo de

Manila, 1979); James Connolly, *Labour in Irish History and the Reconquest of Ireland* (Dublin: Maunsel and Roberts, 1922); William Ryan, *The Irish Labour Movement* (Dublin: Talbot Press, 1919); Emmet O'Connor, *Syndicalism in Ireland, 1917–1923* (Cork: Cork University Press, 1988); Thomas A. Boylan and Timothy P. Foley, *Political Economy and Colonial Ireland* (London and New York: Routledge, 1992).

Nationalisms against the State

1. See Ernest Gellner, *Nations and Nationalism* (Ithaca, NY: Cornell University Press, 1983), p. 125.
2. See Benedict Anderson, *Imagined Communities: Reflections on the Origins and Spread of Nationalism* (London: Verso, 1983).
3. John Breuilly, *Nationalism and the State* (New York: St Martin's Press, 1982).
4. E. J. Hobsbawm, *Nations and Nationalism since 1780: Programme, Myth and Reality* (Cambridge: Cambridge University Press, 1990), p. 164.
5. Tom Nairn, *The Break-up of Britain: Crisis and Neo-Nationalism* (London: New Left Books, 1977), pp. 331–50.
6. Frantz Fanon, *The Wretched of the Earth,* trans. Constance Farrington (New York: Grove Press, 1963), p. 94.
7. I have been inspired in writing this by Alok Yadav's valuable essay, 'Nationalism and Contemporaneity: Political Economy of a Discourse', *Cultural Critique* 26 (Winter 1993–4), pp. 191–229.
8. Gellner, *Nationalism*, p. 4. As the title of *Nationalism and the State* would imply, Breuilly's argument concurs by and large with Gellner's assumption, here at least, in seeing the state as the decisive term for nationalist movements. See Breuilly, esp. pp. 355–9, 374.
9. See E. P. Thompson, 'The Moral Economy of the English Crowd in the Eighteenth Century', *Past and Present* 50 (February 1971), pp. 89–90.
10. Gellner, *Nationalism*, p. 46.
11. Ibid., p. 35.
12. Nairn, *The Break-up of Britain*, pp. 342–3.
13. Ibid., p. 340.
14. Ibid., p. 348.
15. Ibid., p. 349.
16. Ibid., p. 349.
17. Gellner, *Nationalism*, p. 35.
18. See Bipan Chandra, 'Colonialism, Stages of Colonialism, and the Colonial State', *Journal of Contemporary Asia* 10, no. 3 (1980), p. 282, on the focus of the indigenous population as a whole on the state which makes nationalist movements in the colonial state far easier to organize than other kinds of social movement.
19. Among Western theorists of nationalism, Benedict Anderson is one of the few who clearly grasps this dynamic. See *Imagined Communities*, chapter 7.
20. Fanon's essay 'Algeria Unveiled' in *Studies in a Dying Colonialism*, trans. Haakon Chevalier (New York: Grove Press, 1967), analyses the ironic, performative relation of women in the FLN to both modernity and tradition. Lisa Lowe has

analysed such strands in Fanon's thinking in *Critical Terrains: British and French Orientalisms* (Ithaca, NY: Cornell University Press, 1991), pp. 190–2. In my reading of Fanon, and especially in my understanding of the 'contemporaneity' rather than the 'modernity' of heterogeneous social movements at any given time, I have of course learnt greatly from the work of Homi Bhabha. See especially Bhabha's 'DissemiNation: Time, Narrative, and the Margins of the Modern Nation' in Homi Bhabha (ed.), *Nation and Narration* (London: Routledge, 1990), pp. 291–322.

21.   Nairn, *The Break-up of Britain*, p. 340.
22.   Fanon, *The Wretched of the Earth*, p. 204.
23.   Hobsbawm, *Nationalism*, pp. 46–79.
24.   Immanuel Kant, 'The Idea of a Universal History on a Cosmo-Political Plan' in *Works*, vol. 12, trans. Thomas de Quincy (Edinburgh: Adam and Charles Black, 1862), pp. 133-52.
25.   Antonio Gramsci, 'Notes on Italian History' in *Selections from the Prison Notebooks*, trans. and ed. Quintin Hoare and Geoffrey Nowell-Smith (New York: International Publishers, 1971), pp. 52–5; see also Ranajit Guha and Gayatri Chakravorty Spivak (eds.), *Selected Subaltern Studies* (Oxford: Oxford University Press, 1988), pp. 35, 37–43. The relation between Gramsci and subaltern histories in India and Ireland is taken up again in the chapter 'Outside History'.
26.   See Walter Benjamin, 'Theses on the Philosophy of History' in *Illuminations*, ed. Hannah Arendt, trans. Harry Zohn (New York: Schocken, 1969), pp. 260, 262.
27.   Ibid., p. 260.
28.   Ibid., p. 255.
29.   This is clearly a fundamental problematic of subaltern historiography: see in particular Guha's 'The Prose of Counter-Insurgency' (*Selected Subaltern Studies*, pp. 45–86). Rey Ileto's 'Outlines of a Non-Linear Emplotment of Philippine History' in Lisa Lowe and David Lloyd (eds.), *The Politics of Culture in the Shadow of Capital* (Durham, NC: Duke University Press, 1997), pp. 98–131, is a valuable combination of new historical research and formal critique which addresses these questions very subtly. I have attempted some analysis of the incompatibilities between agrarian movements and emergent nationalist ideology in nineteenth-century Ireland in 'Violence and the Constitution of the Novel' in *Anomalous States: Irish Writing and the Post-Colonial Moment* (Dublin: Lilliput Press, 1993), pp. 146–8.
30.   Benjamin, 'Theses on the Philosophy of History', p. 261.
31.   The use of a Freudian vocabulary in this relation, and the implicit congruence thereby established between individual and national history, is unremarkable insofar as Freud himself employs the same metaphors in the inverse direction: national history provides the constant analogy for individual integration and development. See Sigmund Freud, 'The Dissolution of the Oedipal Complex' (1924) and 'Some Psychical Consequences of the Anatomical Distinction Between the Sexes' (1925) in *On Sexuality: Three Essays on the Theory of Sexuality and Other Works*, vol. 7 of The Pelican Freud, ed. Angela Richards, trans. James Strachey (Harmondsworth: Penguin, 1977), esp. p. 341.
32.   See Walter Benjamin, 'Critique of Violence' in *Reflections: Assays, Aphorisms, Autobiographical Writings* ed. Peter Demetz, trans. Edmund Jephcott (New York: Harcourt Brace Jovanovich, 1978), p. 279.

33. The same could be said, *mutatis mutandi*, for ethnic or minority politics in multicultural states like the US or diasporic populations in more 'mono-ethnic' cultures. The destabilizing figure of Leopold Bloom, the wandering Jew, is for this reason one of the things that makes Joyce's *Ulysses* a great counter-nationalist text without it, for that reason, becoming a pro-imperialist one.

34. The term 'modern' is probably misleading here, since some social movements such as agrarian or peasant movements invoke not, say, the discourse of rights but terms which appear traditional (though some, as in the 1798 uprising in Ireland, managed to combine both). The conditions of dislocation, however, produce a transformation of the 'traditional' such that it becomes a new cultural form which responds to 'modernity' in the narrower sense. Opposition to modernity is, then, no less contemporaneous and cannot simply be relegated to the status of outmoded traditionalism. Reynaldo Ileto's *Pasyon and Revolution* is a brilliant analysis of 'contemporaneous' adaptations of the traditional for emancipatory purposes in the context of Philippine resistance to both Spanish and American colonialism.

35. Margaret MacCurtain, 'Women, the Vote and Revolution' in Margaret MacCurtain and Donncha Ó Corrain (eds.), *Women in Irish Society: The Historical Dimension* (Westport, CT: Greenwood Press, 1979), p. 52.

36. For a succinct account of these historiographical categories in Ireland, see Kevin Whelan, 'Come All Ye Blinkered Nationalists: A Post-Revisionist Agenda for Irish History', *Irish Reporter* 2 (2nd Quarter 1991), pp. 24–6. They are comparable to Guha's distinction between colonialist and nationalist historiography in India (*Selected Subaltern Studies*, pp. 37–40). I find it striking that the most innovative new history of Irish nationalism as a movement first emanated from the biographical and historical studies of feminist historians. See, for example, Margaret Ward, *Maud Gonne: Ireland's Joan of Arc* (London: Pandora, 1990); Diana Norman, *Terrible Beauty: The Life of Constance Markievicz* (Dublin: Poolbeg, 1991); Maria Luddy and Cliona Murphy (eds.), *Women Surviving: Studies in Irish Women's History in the 19th and 20th Centuries* (Dublin: Poolbeg, 1990). For an excellent exploration of relations between the sympathetic critique of nationalism and gendered historiography, which focuses on the Indian context, see R. Radhakrishnan, 'Nationalism, Gender and the Narrative of Identity' in Andrew Parker, Mary Russo, Doris Sommer and Patricia Yaeger (eds.), *Nationalisms and Sexualities* (New York: Routledge, 1992), pp. 77–95.

37. MacCurtain, p. 55.

38. Constance Markievicz, *Prison Letters* (London: Longman's Green and Co., 1934), p. 12.

39. Ibid., pp. 246–7. For a discussion of similar discussions in other Irish Marxists of the time, like Aodh de Blacam and James Connolly, see Luke Gibbons, 'Identity Without a Centre: Allegory, History, Irish Nationalism', *Cultural Studies* 6, no. 3 (October 1992), pp. 358–75. His thinking on these issues has been of enormous value to me throughout this essay.

40. See *Prison Letters*, p. 191: 'I don't believe in leaders myself; I had just time to fix up my end before I was "took" and it has had great results with regard to the women.'

41. For details of these movements in the context of modern Filipino history, see Benedict Anderson 'Cacique Democracy in the Philippines: Origins and

Dreams', *New Left Review* 169 (May–June 1988), pp. 3–33; Renato Constantino, 'Identity and Consciousness: The Philippine Experience' in *Journal of Contemporary Asia* 6, no. 1 (1976), pp. 5–29; Norman Lorimer, 'Philippine Communism: An Historical Overview', *Journal of Contemporary Asia* 7, no. 4 (1977), pp. 462–85.

42.   See Lorimer, 'Philippine Communism', p. 477.

43.   Ileto, 'Non-Linear History of the Philippines', pp. 135–6.

44.   Amado Guerrero, 'Specific Characteristics of Our People's War' in *Philippine Society and Revolution* (International Association of Filipino Patriots, 1979), pp. 179–206.

45.   I draw here on the work of a number of Filipina activists and theatre scholars: Rosario Cruz Lucero, *Negros Occidental, 1970–1986: The Fall of the Sugar Industry and the Rise of the People's Theater* (Doctoral Dissertation, University of the Philippines, 1990); Priscelina Patajo-Legasto, *Philippine Contemporary Theater, 1946–1985: A Materialist Analysis* (Doctoral Dissertation, University of the Philippines, 1988); Lulu Torres-Reyes, 'Anticipating Hegemony: Brecht and the Philippines Today', *Makisa* 1, no. 1 (1st Quarter, 1989): pp. 18–19.

46.   Ileto, *Pasyon and Revolution*. PETA's adaptation of 'Yesterday, Today and Tomorrow' (Manila, January 1991) is an allegory of the contemporaneity of cultural forms, taking a turn-of-the-century, seditious and anti-American *zarzuela* and reinflecting it both by culturally diverse elements of performance and by emphasizing its original thematization of the cyclical or repetitive nature of Philippine resistance to colonialism. One consideration here is the tension between contemporary women's activism and nationalist figurations of the feminine: the role of Inang Bayan, mother of the nation, portrayed as perpetually supplicant is in constant tension with the foregrounding of women militants in the 'chorus', thus mobilizing and unsettling the oedipal elements of nationalism.

47.   See, for example, Domingo Castro de Guzman's somewhat intemperate 'Millenarianism and Revolution: A Critique of Reynaldo C. Ileto's *Pasyon and Revolution*', *Journal of Social History* (Institute of Social History, Polytechnic University of the Philippines), vols. 3–4 (n.d.), pp. 31–95.

48.   The recent revival of Irish music, for long enveloped in the dreary drapery of the church- and state-sanctioned *fleadh ceoil* or cultural festival, is an excellent instance of such 'resurgences', determined in part by the encounter with international contemporary music and in part by such phenomena as the encounter between Irish and black young immigrants in the hostile environment of racist Britain and the consequent interaction of cultural styles.

49.   Theodor Adorno, *Negative Dialectics*, trans. E. B. Ashton (New York: Seabury Press, 1973), p. 339.

50.   Louis Althusser, 'Ideology and Ideological State Apparatuses: Notes Towards an Investigation' in *Lenin and Philosophy and Other Essays*, trans. Ben Brewster (New York: Monthly Review Press, 1971), pp. 181–2.

51.   See Gellner, *Nationalism*, pp. 36, 102.

52.   Ibid., p. 34. On Weber's 'classic definition' of the state as 'a human community that (successfully) claims the *monopoly of the legitimate use of physical force* within a given territory', see Ian S. Lustick, *Unsettled States*, p. 3. Emphasis in Lustick.

53.   On this oscillation between the literal and the allegorical, see Luke Gibbons,

'Identity without a Centre' in *Transformations in Irish Culture*, pp. 141–3. On 'Marianne', see T. J. Clark, *The Absolute Bourgeois: Artists and Politics in France, 1848-1851* (Greenwich, CT: New York Graphic Society, 1973), chapters 1 and 2.

Regarding Ireland in a Post-Colonial Frame

1. This essay originated in a talk on Homi K. Bhabha's *Location of Culture*, delivered at the Modern Language Association in San Diego in 1994. I have drawn freely from his thinking, in ways which cannot always be directly attributed. A second and more extended version was delivered at the Graduate Irish Studies Conference at the University of Notre Dame in March 1995. I would like to thank Seamus Deane and the organizers of and participants in that conference for the occasion and for the valuable discussions that have informed this essay.

2. For some work in these directions, see, amongst others, Declan Kiberd's *Inventing Ireland* (Cambridge, MA: Harvard University Press, 1996); the essays by Fredric Jameson, Edward Said and Terry Eagleton in Seamus Deane (ed.), *Nationalism, Colonialism and Literature* (Minneapolis: University of Minnesota Press, 1990); Raymond Crotty, *Ireland in Crisis: A Study in Capitalist Colonial Underdevelopment* (Dingle: Brandon Books, 1986); and Luke Gibbons, 'Identity without a Centre: Allegory, History and Irish Nationalism' in *Transformations in Irish Culture* (Cork: Cork University Press, 1996), pp. 141–3.

3. Anne McClintock, 'The Angel of Progress: Pitfalls of the Term 'Post-Colonialism', *Social Text* 31/32 (1992), p. 85. For further mostly critical discussions of the concept of postcolonialism, see especially Ella Shohat, 'Notes on the "Post-Colonial"', *Social Text* 31/32 (1992), pp. 99–113; Arif Dirlik, 'The Postcolonial Aura: Third World Criticism in the Age of Global Capitalism', *Critical Inquiry* 20 (Winter 1994), pp. 328–56; Anthony Appiah, 'Is the Post- in Postmodernism the Post- in Postcolonial?', *Critical Inquiry* 17 (Winter 1991), pp. 336–57.

4. McClintock, 'Angel of Progress', p. 86.

5. Emmet O'Connor, *Syndicalism in Ireland, 1917–1923* (Cork: Cork University Press, 1988).

6. On the women involved across the various movements of the first quarter of this century, see MacCurtain, 'Women, the Vote and Revolution' in *Women in Irish Society*; Diana Norman, *Terrible Beauty: The Life of Constance Markievicz* (Dublin: Poolbeg, 1991); Margaret Ward, *Maud Gonne: Ireland's Joan of Arc* (London: Pandora, 1990); and Mary Clancy, 'Aspects of Women's Contributions to the Oireachtas Debate in the Irish Free State, 1922–37' in Maria Luddy and Cliona Murphy (eds.) *Women Surviving: Studies in Irish Women's History in the 19th and 20th Centuries* (Dublin: Poolbeg, 1990), pp. 206–32.

7. On the close relation between historiography and the emergence of a modern civil society and its concomitant state form, see Dipesh Chakrabarty, 'Postcoloniality and the Artifice of History: Who Speaks for "Indian" Pasts?', *Representations* 37 (Winter 1992), pp. 1–26. I explore in the chapter 'Outside History' some new directions in Irish history that suggest a set of alternative paradigms.

8. Frantz Fanon, 'The Pitfalls of National Consciousness' in *The Wretched of the Earth*, trans. Constance Farrington (New York: Grove Press, 1968), p. 204.

9. For this phrase, see Karl Marx, 'On the Jewish Question' in *Early Writings*, intro. Lucio Colletti, trans. Rodney Livingstone and Gregor Benton (New York: Vintage, 1974), pp. 211–42.

10. Ranajit Guha, *A Rule of Property for Bengal: An Essay on the Idea of Permanent Settlement* (New Delhi: Orient Longman, 1981), p. 7.

11. Partha Chatterjee, *Nationalist Thought and the Colonial World: A Derivative Discourse?* (London: Zed Books, 1986), chapter 1; Reynaldo C. Ileto, 'Outlines of a Non-Linear Emplotment of Philippine History' in Lisa Lowe and David Lloyd (eds.), *The Politics of Culture in the Shadow of Capital* (Durham, NC: Duke University Press, 1997), pp.99–105; David Lloyd, *Nationalism and Minor Literature: James Clarence Mangan and the Emergence of Irish Cultural Nationalism* (Berkeley: University of California Press, 1987), chapter 2; and Declan Kiberd, *Inventing Ireland: The Literature of a Modern Nation* (Cambridge, MA: Harvard University Press, 1995), pp. 551–61.

12. Michel Foucault, 'Governmentality' in Graham Burchell, Colin Gordon and Peter Miller (eds.), *The Foucault Effect: Studies in Governmentality* (London: Harvester Wheatsheaf, 1991), pp. 87–104.

13. Benjamin, 'Theses on the Philosophy of History' in *Illuminations*, ed. Hannah Arendt, trans. Harry Zohn (New York: Schocken, 1969), pp. 254–64.

14. Gramsci, 'Notes on Italian History' in *Selections from the Prison Notebooks*, ed. and trans. Quintin Hoare and Geoffrey Nowell-Smith (New York: International Publishers, 1971), pp. 52–5. Something of Gramsci's tendency survives in the early subaltern work which Spivak has critiqued in 'Deconstructing Historiography' for its insistence on pursuing the proto-political *consciousness* of subaltern groups; see that essay in Ranajit Guha and Gayatri Chakravorty Spivak (eds.), *Selected Subaltern Studies* (Oxford: Oxford University Press, 1988), pp. 3–52.

15. See Fanon, 'On National Culture' in *Wretched of the Earth*, pp. 206–48, and Benedict Anderson, *Imagined Communities: Reflections on the Origins and Spread of Nationalism*, rev. ed. (London: Verso, 1991), chapter 7.

16. Ileto, 'Outlines of a Non-Linear Emplotment of Philippine History', pp. 115–19 and 122–4.

17. See Charles Townsend, *Political Violence in Ireland: Government and Resistance since 1848* (Oxford: Oxford University Press, 1983), pp. 8–9.

18. See further, on the agrarian movements, 'Violence and the Constitution of the Novel' in Lloyd, *Anomalous States*, pp. 125–62.

19. For an analysis of some of the modes of surveillance and repression deployed in Northern Ireland, see Carol Ackroyd, Karen Margolis, Jonathan Rosenhead and Tim Shallice, *The Technology of Political Control*, 2nd. ed. (London: Pluto, 1980), esp. pp. 40–2. See also Steve Wright, 'An Assessment of the New Technologies of Repression' in Marjo Hoefnagels (ed.), *Repression and Repressive Violence* (Amsterdam: Swets and Zeitlinger, 1977), and Paddy Hillyard, 'The Normalization of Special Powers: From Northern Ireland to Britain' in Phil Scranton (ed.), *Law, Order and the Authoritarian State: Readings in Critical Criminology* (Milton Keynes: Open University Press, 1987).

20. On the processes of state censorship that have profoundly affected public understanding of Northern Ireland, see Liz Curtis, *Ireland: the Propaganda War. The British Media and the Battle for Hearts and Minds* (London: Pluto, 1984).

21. For accounts of the 'strong state' and its extension, see the works cited in n. 18
     above. For Brigadier Frank Kitson's writings, see his *Low Intensity Operations:
     Subversion, Insurgency and Peace-Keeping* (London: Faber, 1971) and *Bunch of
     Five* (London: Faber and Faber, 1977), an account of his involvement in several
     postwar colonial campaigns, including Kenya, Malaya, Muscat and Oman, and
     Cyprus. On the general logic of counter-insurgency, also written from the per-
     spective of the military and the state, see Andrew M. Scott, *Insurgency* (Chapel
     Hill: University of North Carolina Press, 1970). For some theoretically sugges-
     tive exceptions to this tendency to understand contemporary Northern Irish
     conditions always by reference to their implications for the British state, see
     Allen Feldman, *Formations of Violence: The Narrative of the Body and Political Ter-
     ror in Northern Ireland* (Chicago: University of Chicago Press, 1991); Barbara
     Harlow, ' "Beyond the Pale": Strip-Searching and Hunger Strikes in Northern
     Ireland' in *Barred: Women, Writing and Political Detention* (Hanover: Wesleyan
     University Press/University Press of New England, 1992), pp. 78–100; and Beg-
     ona Aretxaga, 'Dirty Protest: Symbolic Overdetermination and Gender in
     Northern Ireland Ethnic Violence', *Ethos* 23, no. 2 (1995), pp. 123–48.
22. See Kitson, *Bunch of Five*, pp. 287–9.
23. Seamus Heaney has encapsulated this notion of secrecy in citing the colloquial
     wisdom, 'Whatever you say, say nothing', in the poem of that name in *North*
     (London: Faber and Faber, 1975), pp. 57–60. Feldman, *Formations of Violence*,
     pp. 56–9, explores the resonant semantics of 'telling' as an interpretive practice
     that works across the opacity of Northern Irish culture.
24. For a brief overview of the history of segregated settlement of Belfast, see A. T.
     Q. Stewart, *The Narrow Ground: The Roots of Conflict in Ulster* rev. ed. (London:
     Faber and Faber, 1989), pp. 143–5; for Fanon, see *Wretched of the Earth*, pp.
     38–9.
25. Raymond Williams, *The Country and the City* (New York: Oxford University
     Press, 1973), pp. 165–82.
26. The restructuring of Belfast of recent years is reminiscent of Mike Davis's
     description of the symptomatic postmodern architecture of contemporary Los
     Angeles, which resembles a 'besieged landscape' and is 'governed by a Haus-
     mannian logic of social control' precisely where it is most given over to con-
     sumer fetishism. See his 'Urban Renaissance and the Spirit of Postmodernism',
     New Left Review 151 (May–June 1985), pp. 112–13.
27. See Brian Campbell, Laurence McKeown and Felim O'Hagan (eds.), *Nor Meekly
     Serve Our Time: The H-Block Struggle, 1976–1981* (Belfast: Beyond the Pale Pub-
     lications, 1994), p. 2. This account, by the prisoners themselves, provides an
     exceptional basis for understanding the intersection of bodily and adaptive
     technological means of resistance within the reduced space of the prison cells
     that does much to counter the media-disseminated representation of the prison
     struggle as predicated on atavistic republican ideologies.
28. On the mural work of contemporary Belfast, see Bill Rolston, *Drawing Support:
     Murals in Northern Ireland* (Belfast: Beyond the Pale, 1992) and 'The Writing on
     the Wall: The Murals of Gerry Kelly', *Irish Reporter* 2 (1991).
29. Ciaran Carson, *Belfast Confetti* (Winston-Salem: Wake Forest University Press,
     1989).
30. 'Question Time' in *Belfast Confetti*, pp. 58–9.

31. 'Intelligence' in *Belfast Confetti*, p. 78. Original emphasis.
32. Ibid., p. 78.
33. Cf. Wright, 'Technologies of Repression', p. 135: 'Technology in operation may be considered to consist of two components, namely, software and hardware. The software in this context may be considered as a programme of systematic logic designed to plan and orientate the other structural components in a functional way.'
34. 'Intelligence' in *Belfast Confetti*, p. 79.
35. Ibid., p. 79
36. Ibid., p. 80.
37. Ibid., p. 81.
38. 'Brick' in *Belfast Confetti*, p. 72.

True Stories

1. I derive this reading from a talk given by Luke Gibbons at the Irish Cultural Center, San Francisco, October 1994.
2. A. T. Q. Stewart, *The Narrow Ground: The Roots of Conflict in Ulster*, rev. ed. (London: Faber and Faber, 1989).
3. J. Bowyer Bell, *The Irish Troubles: A Generation of Violence, 1967–1992* (New York: St Martin's Press, 1993).
4. Ranajit Guha, 'The Prose of Counter-Insurgency' in Ranajit Guha and Gayatri Chakravorty Spivak (eds.), *Selected Subaltern Studies* (Oxford: Oxford University Press, 1988), pp. 45–86.
5. I derive this model from Kant's *Conflict of the Faculties* where, in the second essay, on the conflict between the faculty of law and the faculty of philosophy, the function of the historian/philosopher is to draw as *spectator* rather than participant the world historical meaning from an event like the French Revolution; specifically, the lesson drawn from the violence of that event is the necessity for the constitutionally regulated state. See Kant, *Conflict of the Faculties/Der Streit der Fakultaeten* (1798), trans. and intro. Mary J. Gregor (New York: Abaris, 1979), pp. 151–61.
6. Though this is not the occasion to develop this line of inquiry, I should say that my reflections on the problems of thinking the historical event outside either causal or paradigmatic forms has been influenced by two texts in particular: Joel Fineman's analysis of the structures of historical narrative in 'The History of the Anecdote' in *The Subjectivity Effect in Western Literature: Essays towards the Release of Shakespeare's Will* (Cambridge, MA: MIT Press, 1991), pp. 59–87, and Gilles Deleuze's distinctions between sense and event in *The Logic of Sense*, ed. Constantin V. Boundas, trans. Mark Lester with Charles Stivale (New York: Columbia University Press, 1990).
7. For an excellent survey of the coverage of Northern Ireland in the British and Irish press, see Philip Elliott, *Reporting Northern Ireland: A Study of News in Great Britain, Northern Ireland and the Republic of Ireland* in *Ethnicity and the Media: an Analysis of Media Reporting in the United Kingdom, Canada and Ireland*, Part III (Paris: UNESCO, 1977), pp. 263–376.
8. Stewart, *Narrow Ground*, p. 9.

9.   Ibid., esp. pp. 145–54.

10.   Ibid., p. 113.

11.   Ibid., pp. 115–16.

12.   Stewart's figures here correspond with those that Ileto finds in Philippine histories of the bandit. See the previous chapter for a discussion of these.

13.   For Matthew Arnold's remark, see *Culture and Anarchy*, ed. J. Dover Wilson (Cambridge: Cambridge University Press, 1984), p. 96. F. S. L. Lyons' well-known collection of essays on nineteenth-century Ireland, *Culture and Anarchy in Ireland*, is aptly but quite unironically so entitled. For a fuller discussion of the differential model invoked here, see David Lloyd and Paul Thomas, *Culture and the State* (New York: Routledge, 1997).

14.   Stewart, *Narrow Ground*, p. 16.

15.   Signal among these contradictions, which are too numerous to address in full here, is that which emerges from the fundamental assertion that 'violence is endemic' in Ireland. The inescapable implication, that it is an ethnic characteristic, an assumption certainly embedded in his sources, runs up against the fact that violence in Ireland has always involved the question of conquest and occupation and against the fact that, as Stewart himself takes pains to show, the forms of violence his own argument distinguishes are equally typical of both conflicting ethnic groups. A further point is that Stewart never addresses the role of the state in producing the violence which it then appears to put down.

16.   See, for some examples, Dipesh Chakrabarty, 'Postcoloniality and the Artifice of History: Who Speaks for "Indian" Pasts?', *Representations* 37 (Winter 1992), pp. 1–26; Partha Chatterjee's *The Nation and Its Fragments: Colonial and Postcolonial Histories* (Princeton, NJ: Princeton University Press, 1993); and the essays collected in Kum Kum Sangari and Sudesh Vaid (eds.), *Recasting Women: Essays in Indian Colonial History* (New Delhi: Kali for Women, 1989).

17.   See, for example, the extended narrative of the Yank historian's visit to Belfast for a Republican Club protest, pp. 13–17.

18.   My understanding of the hunger strikes is greatly indebted to a number of works, including: Allen Feldman, *Formations of Violence: The Narrative of the Body and Political Terror in Northern Ireland* (Chicago: University of Chicago Press, 1991); Barbara Harlow, *Barred: Women, Writing and Political Detention* (Hanover: Wesleyan University Press/University Press of New England, 1992); David Beresford, *Ten Men Dead: The Story of the 1981 Irish Hunger Strike* (New York: Atlantic Monthly Press, 1987); Begonia Aretxaga, 'Dirty Protest: Symbolic Overdetermination and Gender in Northern Ireland Ethnic Violence', *Ethos* 23, no. 2 (1995); and especially Brian Campbell, Laurence McKeown and Felim O'Hagan (eds.), *Nor Meekly Serve Our Time: The H-Block Struggle, 1976–1981* (Belfast: Beyond the Pale, 1994), a narrative compiled by ex-prisoners themselves.

19.   Bowyer Bell, *The Irish Troubles*, p. 625.

20.   Ibid., p. 609.

21.   On the fetish character of the stereotype, see Homi Bhabha, 'The Other Question: Stereotype, Discrimination and the Discourse of Colonialism' in *Locations of Culture* (New York: Routledge, 1996), pp. 66–84.

22.   I use this expression in the sense developed by Michel Foucault to designate both the institutions of the modern state and the forms of subjectivity they pro-

duce. See his essay 'Governmentality' in Graham Burchell, Colin Gordon and Peter Miller (eds.), *The Foucault Effect: Studies in Governmentality* (London: Harvester Wheatsheaf, 1991), pp. 87–104.

23. Bowyer Bell, *The Irish Troubles*, p. 585.

24. Jurgen Habermas has discussed some of the tendencies towards the decline of the participatory public sphere and the emergence of forms of corporate and technocratic state in 'The Public Sphere', translated in Chandra Mukerji and Michael Schudson (eds.), *Rethinking Popular Culture: Contemporary Perspectives in Cultural Studies* (Berkeley: University of California Press, 1991), pp. 398–404. It is of course questionable whether such an ideal form of public sphere as he theorizes ever existed even virtually in Ireland, let alone elsewhere. See also the previous chapter for some analysis of the ramifications of surveillance and for references to the literature on the technology involved.

25. See Aristotle, *On the Art of Fiction: An English Translation of the Poetics*, 2nd impression (Cambridge: Cambridge University Press, 1959), p. 29. The terms for verisimilitude that I am using here and throughout this essay are derived from Tsvetan Todorov, 'Introduction to Verisimilitude' in *The Poetics of Prose*, trans. Richard Howard (Ithaca, NY: Cornell University Press, 1977).

26. In addition to referring to the film itself, I refer throughout to Neil Jordan's screenplay in *The Neil Jordan Reader* (New York: Vintage, 1993).

27. See Feldman, *Formations of Violence, passim.*

28. The reality effect of the hostage-taking probably derives on the one hand from a conflation of IRA 'terrorism' with Middle Eastern groups for whom hostage-taking has been an important and well-publicized tactic, and, on the other, with a series of 'generic' references, including Frank O'Connor's much less romantic short story 'Guests of the Nation' and Brendan Behan's play *The Hostage*.

29. John Hill's essay, 'Images of Violence' in Kevin Rockett, Luke Gibbons and John Hill (eds.), *Cinema and Ireland* (London: Routledge, 1988), serves also as an excellent introduction to this tendency in representation of 'terrorism'. I will make extensive use of Hill's work in what follows.

30. On the long and persistent traditions of anti-Irish racism, including this modern version, see Liz Curtis, *Nothing But the Same Old Story: The Roots of Anti-Irish Racism* (London: Information on Ireland, 1984).

31. See especially Edward Said, 'Identity, Negation and Violence', *New Left Review* 171 (1988), pp. 16–30.

32. Hill, 'Images', p. 145.

33. Ibid., pp. 179–80.

34. Frantz Fanon, *Black Skin, White Masks*, trans. Charles Lam Markmann, foreword by Homi Bhabha (London: Pluto, 1986), pp. 10–11. I have discussed the cultural regulation of racial categories in 'Race under Representation', *Oxford Literary Review* 13 (Spring 1991), pp. 62–94. We will return at the end of this paper to the ambiguity as to the meaning of the term 'Man' to which the colonized seek to be adequate.

35. In what follows, I draw freely and extensively from Hill, 'Images', and also from Harlow, *Barred*, pp. 87–9.

36. Hill, 'Images', p. 147

37. Ibid., p. 155.

38. Ibid., p. 155.

39.   Ibid., p. 159.
40.   On relations between *The Crying Game* and Hitchcock, see Peter N. Chumo II, 'The Crying Game *and* Vertigo: The Quest for Identity', *Bright Lights* 11 (Fall 1993), pp. 26–9, and Mark Simpson, *Male Impersonators: Men Performing Masculinity* (London: Cassell, 1994), pp. 173–4.
41.   For an excellent reading of both the sexual and racial politics of *The Crying Game*, see Kristin Handler, 'Sexing *The Crying Game*: Difference, Identity, Ethics', *Film Quarterly* 47 (Spring 1994), pp. 31–42. See also Simpson, *Male Impersonators*, chapter 8, pp. 164–76; Frann Michel, 'Racial and Sexual Politics in *The Crying Game*' and David Lugowski, 'Genre Conventions and Visual Style in *The Crying Game*', both in *Cineaste* 20.1 (1993), pp. 30, 31, pp. 30–5. I find my reading of the film intersecting with all these essays at different points.
42.   In this scene, Fergus's obsession with doing what Jody did with Dil is also foregrounded. But the fact that Fergus here has a singular object of imitation does not detract from the larger citational structure of gendered desire. My arguments in this section are clearly indebted to Judith Butler's *Gender Trouble: Feminism and the Subversion of Identity* (London: Routledge, 1990).
43.   See Georg Lukacs, *Theory of the Novel*, trans. Anna Bostock (Cambridge, MA: MIT Press, 1971).
44.   See Freud, 'The Dissolution of the Oedipus Complex' (1924) and his *Three Essays on the Theory of Sexuality* (1905) in *On Sexuality: Three Essays on the Theory of Sexuality and Other Works*, Pelican Freud Library, vol. 7, ed. Angela Richards, trans. James Strachey (Harmondsworth: Penguin, 1977).
45.   The formulation 'The desire of the man is for the woman; the desire of the woman is for the desire of the man' may now be best known from Lacan, but it has a specifically Irish and prior source in Yeats's note to *The Wanderings of Oisin* in *Collected Poems* (London, Macmillan, 1961), p. 526. Given Jordan's artful allusiveness, it seems probable that Fergus's name echoes the famous Celtic lover-king of Yeats's early verse.
46.   We can read Fergus's 'shearing' of Dil as enacting his desire to normalize his relation to her on the axis of a father–son relationship, predicated on care and protection, as well as a sublimating 'castration' of her as object of desire. Fergus becomes Dil's father as Dil becomes not only a visual repetition of Jody in cricket gear but 'manifestly' a boy. Their relation at this point also becomes subject to the most rigorous of all incest taboos, reinforcing Fergus's proscription of sexual relations. This is not of course to say that breach of that taboo is impossible, but only to echo Stephen Dedalus's interestingly hedged and arch formulation in *Ulysses*: 'They are sundered by a bodily shame so steadfast that the criminal annals of the world, stained with all other incests and bestialities, hardly record its breach.' (*Ulysses*, ed. Hans Walter Gabler [New York: Random House, 1986], p. 170.)
47.   On conditions for relatives of Irish prisoners in British gaols, see Carol Coulter, *Web of Punishment*.
48.   *Jordan Reader*, pp. 240–41.
49.   Cited in *Washington Post*, February 18, 1993.
50.   Cf. Eileen MacDonald, *Shoot the Women First* (New York: Random House, 1991), p. xix.
51.   See Thomas Laqueur, "Making New Rules", in *Threepenny Review* (March 1993), p. 32.

52.   It is hard not to be struck by the correspondence between the violent death of Jude in *The Crying Game* and the excess of force used in the killing of Mairead Farrell in Gibraltar which Harlow cites at length (*Barred*, pp. 78–9). In her study of 'women committed to violence', *Shoot the Women First* – a title which indeed alludes to British counter-insurgency policy – Eileen MacDonald discusses the peculiar anxiety which the 'monstrousness' of the figure of the woman terrorist provokes. Yet, despite extensive interviews with women involved in insurgent groups, even this writer is unable quite to shake off the baseless image of the 'pathological' terrorist.

53.   I have discussed such a moment, and its relation to the traditional aesthetic distribution of the sublime and the beautiful, in 'The Poetic of Politics: Yeats and the Founding of the State' in *Anomalous States*, pp. 72–3.

54.   See Matthew Arnold, *The Study of Celtic Literature* in R. H. Super (ed.), *The Complete Prose Works of Matthew Arnold*, vol. 3, *Lectures and Essays in Criticism*. I have discussed this essay extensively in *Nationalism and Minor Literature: James Clarence Mangan and the Emergence of Irish Cultural Nationalism* (Berkeley and Los Angeles: University of California Press, 1987), pp. 6–13. For further work on the 'feminization' of the Irish, see David Cairns and Sean Richards, *Writing Ireland: Colonialism, Nationalism and Culture* (Manchester: Manchester University Press, 1988), chapter 3.

55.   I allude here to Butler's compelling arguments in *Gender Trouble*, pp. 57–72.

56.   *Jordan reader*, p. 267.

57.   Cf. Handler, 'Sexing *The Crying Game*', pp. 34–5. I should remark that my argument differs from Handler's in seeing Fergus's 'humanization' as an emergence from an initially racialized feminization into mature manhood. His initial violence is Irish, feminine and underdeveloped, rather than masculine.

58.   Cf. Simpson, *Male Impersonators*, p. 174.

59.   Again, cf. Handler, 'Sexing *The Crying Game*', pp. 38–40.

60.   See Ashis Nandy, *The Intimate Enemy: Loss and Recovery of Self Under Colonialism* (Oxford: Oxford University Press, 1983), pp. 56–62. For some of Gramsci's strictures on folklore as a mode, again, of 'fragmentary and episodic' consciousness, see *Selections from the Prison Notebooks of Antonio Gramsci*, ed. and trans. Quintin Hoare and Geoffrey Nowell-Smith (New York: International Publishers, 1971), pp. 30–1, 33–5, 362, 419. For further criticism of Gramsci's reading of popular or folk culture, see Jose Rabasa, 'Of Zapatismo: Reflections on the Folkloric and the Impossible in a Subaltern Insurrection' in Lisa Lowe and David Lloyd (eds.), *The Politics of Culture in the Shadow of Capitalism* (Durham, NC: Duke University Press, 1997), pp. 399–431.

Outside History

1.   On parallels between Ireland and India, see S. B Cooke, *Imperial Affinities: Nineteenth-Century Analogies and Exchanges Between India and Ireland* (New Delhi: Sage, 1993), and Raymond Crotty, *Ireland in Crisis: A Study in Capitalist Colonial Underdevelopment* (Dingle: Brandon Books, 1986). I use the term 'subalternity effect' by analogy with the late Joel Fineman's use of the term 'subjectivity effect' in relation to the emergence of the Western subject, as he argues, in literature

and especially in Shakespeare. See Fineman, *The Subjectivity Effect in Western Literature: Essays towards the Release of Shakespeare's Will* (Cambridge, MA: MIT Press, 1991).

2.   See Gayatri Chakravorty Spivak, 'Deconstructing Historiography' in Ranajit Guha and Gayatri Chakravorty Spivak (eds.), *Selected Subaltern Studies*, (Oxford: Oxford University Press, 1988), pp. 5–15. I have learnt much from this essay, but it will be clear to the reader that the notion of an 'effect' here is not directed towards what Spivak calls a 'subject-effect', but rather to a concept of agency and the event which is not predicated upon a singular historical subject taken as cause of the event. This is, therefore, after both Fineman and Spivak, a turn on the term which has the task of displacing the historical explanatory power of 'cause and effect' paradigms.

3.   See Raymond Williams, *Marxism and Literature* (Oxford: Oxford University Press, 1977), 121–7.

4.   Guha and Spivak, *Selected Subaltern Studies*, p. 35.

5.   Edmund Curtis, *A History of Ireland* (London: Methuen, 1961), p. vi.

6.   For a fuller survey of this tradition and its recent critics, see Tom Dunne, 'New Histories: Beyond "Revisionism"', *The Irish Review* 12 (Spring/Summer 1992), pp. 1–12. For a defence of revisionism, see Michael Laffan's essay 'Insular Attitudes: The Revisionists and their Critics' in Mairin Ní Dhonnchadha and Theo Dorgan (eds.), *Revising the Rising* (Derry: Field Day, 1991), pp. 106–21; for critical positions, especially in relation to Roy Foster's recent work, see Seamus Deane, 'Wherever Green Is Read' in Ní Donnchadha and Dorgan, pp. 91–105; Brian P. Murphy, 'Past Events and Present Politics: Roy Foster's *Modern Ireland*' in Daltún O'Ceallaigh (ed.), *Reconsiderations of Irish History and Culture* (Dublin: Leirmheas, 1994), pp. 72–93, and Donal McCartney, 'History Revisions: Good and Bad' in ibid., pp. 134–56.

7.   See, Dunne, 'New Histories', and A. T. Q. Stewart, 'A Scholar and a Gentleman', interview with Hiram Morgan, *History Ireland* (Summer 1993), pp. 55–8.

8.   For a useful survey of such new histories and the current historical debates, see the section 'New Histories: Visions and Revisions' of *The Irish Review* 12 (Spring/Summer 1992).

9.   See Hume's 'Time for all sectors to reflect deeply on the legacy of Irish nationalism' in the *Irish Times*, 13 April 1994. For an overview of 'regional solutions', see Richard Kearney and Robin Wilson, 'Northern Ireland's Future as a European Region', *The Irish Review* 15 (Spring 1994), pp. 51–69.

10.   For a critique of the notion of 'incomplete modernity' in the Indian context, see Dipesh Chakrabarty, "Postcoloniality and the Artifice of History: Who Speaks of 'Indian' Pasts?", *Representations* 37 (Winter 1990), pp. 1–26.

11.   For some of the contradictions attendant on the close relation between sectarianism and the secular claims of the Northern Irish state, see Jennifer Todd, 'The Limits of Britishness', *The Irish Review* 5 (Autumn 1988), pp. 11–16.

12.   See Cliona Murphy, 'Women's History, Feminist History, or Gender History?', *The Irish Review* 12 (Spring/Summer 1992), pp. 21–6.

13.   See Maria Luddy and Cliona Murphy (eds.), *Women Surviving: Studies in Irish Women's History in the 19th and 20th Centuries* (Dublin: Poolbeg, 1990), p. 3.

14.   See, for example, the pioneering studies in ibid., and the editors' comments, p. 2; Mary Cullen, 'History Women and History Men: The Politics of Women's

History' in Daltún O'Ceallaigh, *Reconsiderations of Irish History and Culture*, pp. 113–33. See also the more recent collections, Mary Cullen and Maria Luddy (eds.), *Women, Power and Consciousness in Nineteenth-Century Ireland* (Dublin: Attic Press, 1995); Maryann Gialanella Valiulis and Mary O'Dowd (eds.), *Women and Irish Women History: Essays in Honour of Margaret MacCurtain* (Dublin: Wolfhound Press, 1997).

15. Kevin Whelan pointed out to me that this disdain for local histories is closely related to the traditional historiographer's suspicion of non-written sources such as ballads and tales, which are, nonetheless, crucial to subaltern historiography.

16. For some instances of these conjunctions between cultural studies and new history, see Cheryl Herr (ed.), *For the Land They Loved: Irish Political Melodramas, 1890–1925* (New York: Syracuse University Press, 1991), David Lloyd, 'Adulteration and the Nation' in *Anomalous States: Irish Writing and the Post-Colonial Moment* (Dublin: Lilliput Press, 1993); Kevin Rockett, "Disguising Dependence: Separatism and Foreign Mass Culture", *Circa* 49 (Jan/Feb 1990), pp. 20–5; Emmet O'Connor, *Syndicalism in Ireland, 1917–1923* (Cork: Cork University Press, 1988); Liam Cahill, *Forgotten Revolution: Limerick Soviet, 1919, a Threat to British Power in Ireland* (Dublin: O'Brien Press, 1990); and also the texts on women's history cited in note 14.

17. See E. J. Hobsbawm, *Nations and Nationalism Since 1780: Programme, Myth and Reality* (Cambridge: Cambridge University Press, 1990), and the discussion of him and other critics of nationalism in the chapter 'Nationalisms against the State'.

18. Luke Gibbons, 'Identity without a Centre' in *Transformations in Irish Culture* (Cork: Cork University Press, 1996), pp. 142–4.

19. Walter Benjamin, 'Theses on the Philosophy of History' in *Illuminations*, ed. Hannah Arendt, trans. Harry Zohn (New York: Schocken, 1969), p. 255.

20. See Ranajit Guha, 'The Prose of Counter-Insurgency' in Guha and Spivak (eds.), *Selected Subaltern Studies*, pp. 45–86, for a magisterial analysis of the formal elements of dominant historiography. I would want to suggest here, in the spirit of Ileto's work on the *pasyon*, that the formal analysis of popular or subaltern cultural forms suggests equally the outline of other semiotics of organization and movement. See Reynaldo C. Ileto, *Pasyon and Revolution: Popular Movements in the Philippines, 1840–1910* (Manila: Ateneo de Manila, 1979).

21. It should also be remarked that the often unintended tendency of the criticism of both states is to legitimate unionist arguments for preferring the association with a 'more modern' British civil society to unification with the conservative Irish Republic.

22. For some recent work on 1798 and the United Irishmen, see for example Jim Smyth, *The Men of No Property: Irish Radicals and Popular Politics in the Late Eighteenth Century* (London: Macmillan, 1992); D. Dickson et al. (eds.), *The United Irishmen: Republicanism, Radicalism and Rebellion* (Dublin: Lilliput, 1993); and, especially, Kevin Whelan, *The Tree of Liberty: Radicalism, Catholicism and the Construction of Irish Identity, 1760–1830* (Cork: Cork University Press, 1996).

23. Continuing resistance by conservative if rural-based parties to the Irish Labour Party's moves to extend voting rights to recent emigrants is a pragmatic acknowledgement both of the radicalizing effects of emigration on many and of

the way in which the emigration of the working classes has historically consolidated conservatism in 'independent' Ireland. On patterns of emigration and their relation to Irish politics, see Jim MacLaughlin's essays, 'Ireland: An "Emigrant Nursery" in the World Economy', *International Quarterly Review* 31, no. 1 (1993), pp. 149–70; 'Place, Politics, and Culture in Nation-Building Ulster: Constructing Nationalist Hegemony in Post-Famine Donegal', *Canadian Review of Studies in Nationalism* 20, nos. 1–2 (1993), pp. 97–111; 'Social Characteristics and Destination of Recent Emigrants from Selected Regions in the West of Ireland', *Geoforum* 22, no. 3 (1991), pp. 319–31. Irish music, which has in any case historically emerged from and been transformed by the experience of emigration from the mid-nineteenth century, continues to be an excellent register of the radicalizing potential of migration. For two notable instances, see the London-based group, Marxman, *33 Revolutions per Minute* (London: Phonogram, 1993), and the New York-based Black 47, *Fire of Freedom* (New York: SBK, 1993).

24.   Timothy Guinnane discusses the rates of female emigration at several points in his study, *The Vanishing Irish: Household, Migration, and the Rural Economy, 1850–1914* (Princeton NJ: Princeton University Press, 1997).

25.   For a survey of the history of women's labour in modern Ireland, see Jennifer Beale, *Women in Ireland: Voices of Change* (Bloomington: Indiana University Press, 1987). On these trends globally, see Swasti Mitter, *Common Fate, Common Bond* (London: Pluto Press, 1986).

26.   Lisa Lowe and I have discussed relations between traditionalist, patriarchal nation-states and global capitalism in the introduction to *The Politics of Culture in the Shadow of Capitalism* (Durham, NC: Duke University Press, 1997).

27.   See Clara Connolly, 'Culture or Citizenship? Notes from the "Gender and Colonialism" Conference, Galway, Ireland, May 1992', *Feminist Review* 44 (Summer 1993), p. 109.

28.   Raymond Williams, *Marxism and Literature* (Oxford: Oxford University Press, 1977), pp. 128–35.

The Recovery of Kitsch

An earlier version of this essay was published in the catalogue, *Distant Relations: Chicano, Irish, Mexican Art and Critical Writing*, Trisha Ziff (ed.), (New York: Smart Art Press, 1996), pp. 146–155.

1.   See Benedict Anderson, *Imagined Communities: Reflections on the Origins and Spread of Nationalism* (London: Verso, 1991).

2.   See Franco Moretti, *The Way of the World: The Bildungsroman in European Culture* (London: Verso, 1987), p. 36. Celeste Olalquiaga has pointed out how much the same holds true for religious kitsch; see her *Megalopolis: Contemporary Cultural Sensibilities* (Minnesota: University of Minnesota Press, 1992), pp. 42–4.

3.   On Loos's writings on kitsch, see Miriam Gusevich, 'Decoration and Decorum, Adolf Loos's Critique of Kitsch', *New German Critique* 43 (Winter 1988), pp. 97–123.

4.   Theodor W. Adorno, 'Commodity Music Analysed' in *Quasi Una Fantasia: Essays on Modern Music*, trans. Rodney Livingstone (London: Verso, 1992), p. 44. I

have of course been inspired here equally by Walter Benjamin's famous essay, 'The Work of Art in the Age of Mechanical Reproduction', and will subsequently draw much from his masterful *Origins of German Tragedy* for my reflections on kitsch, melancholy and allegory.

5. Adorno, 'Commodity Music', p. 50.

6. See, for example, Cherrie Moraga, 'A Long Line of *Vendidas*' in *Loving in the War Years: Lo que nunca paso por sus labios* (Boston: South End Press, 1983); Norma Alarcon, "Tradutora, Traditora: A Paradigmatic Figure of Chicana Feminism", in *Cultural Critique* 13 (Fall, 1989), pp. 57–87; and the artwork of Amalia Mesa-Bains, Yolanda M. Lopez or Ester Hernandez. This kind of work is discussed in Olalquiaga, *Megalopolis*, pp. 46–55.

7. Quoted by Bill Rolston in 'The Writing on the Wall: The Murals of Gerry Kelly', *Irish Reporter* 2 (1991), p. 15.

8. This version of reappropriated kitsch is what Celeste Olalquiaga terms 'third-degree kitsch' in *Megalopolis*, pp. 46–55.

9. For a brief and insightful analysis of Connolly's theory and practices, see Bernard Ransom, *James Connolly* [incomplete?]. For Emilio Zapata and the contemporary Zapatistas, see John Ross, *Rebellion from the Roots: Indian Uprisings in Chiapas* (Monroe, ME: Common Courage Press, 1995).

10. For an elaboration of these processes in the US context, see Lisa Lowe, *Immigrant Acts: On Asian American Cultural Politics* (Durham, NC: Duke University Press, 1996), pp. 21–9 and *passim*. It will be evident that my thinking here owes much to Lowe's work.

11. On this phenomenon, see Etienne Balibar and Immanuel Wallerstein, *Race, Nation, Class: Ambiguous Identities* (London: Verso, 1991), p. 5.

Epilogue

1. Mary Corcoran, 'New York, New York', *Irish Reporter* 1 (1st Quarter 1991), p. 6.

2. Declan Kiberd, 'Emigration: The Same Old Story?', *Irish Reporter* 1 (First Quarter 1991), pp. 3–5.

3. Catriona Ruane, 'A Memoir of Development', *Irish Reporter* 12 (Fourth Quarter 1993), pp. 19–20.

4. Joseph Lee made these remarks in 'Emigration: The Irish Experience', a talk to the Center for Western European Studies, U.C. Berkeley, October 1994.

5. For some sources for the history of these processes, see: Theodore Allen, *The Invention of the White Race* (London: Verso, 1994); Noel Ignatiev, *How the Irish Became White* (New York, Routledge, 1997); and David Roediger, *The Wages of Whiteness: Race and the Making of the American Working Class* (London: Verso, 1991).

6. Bernadette Devlin McAliskey, 'Where Are We Now in the Peace Process?', *Irish Reporter* 21 (February 1996), pp. 23–8.

BIBLIOGRAPHY

Achebe, Chinua, *Things Fall Apart*. London: Heinemann, 1958.

Ackroyd, Carol, Karen Margolis, Jonathan Rosenhead and Tim Shallice, *The Technology of Political Control*. 2nd edition. London: Pluto, 1980.

Adorno, Theodor, *Negative Dialectics*. Translated by E. B. Ashton. New York: Seabury Press, 1973.

—— *Quasi una Fantasia. Essays on Modern Music*, p. 130, n. 4.

Alarcon, Norma, "Tradutora, Traditora: A Paradigmatic Figure of Chicana Feminism" in *Cultural Critique* 14, (Fall 1989): 57–87.

Allen, Theodore, *The Invention of the White Race*. London: Verso, 1994.

Althusser, Louis, 'Ideology and Ideological State Apparatuses: Notes towards an Investigation' in *Lenin and Philosophy and other Essays*. Translated by Ben Brewster. New York: Monthly Review Press, 1971.

Anderson, Benedict, *Imagined Communities: Reflections on the Origins and Spread of Nationalism*. London: Verso, 1983.

—— 'Cacique Democracy in the Philippines: Origins and Dreams', *New Left Review* 169 (May–June 1988): 3–33.

Appiah, Anthony, 'Is the Post- in Postmodernism the Post- in Postcolonial?', *Critical Inquiry* 17 (Winter 1991): 336–57.

Aretxaga, Begona, 'Dirty Protest: Symbolic Overdetermination and Gender in Northern Ireland Ethnic Violence', *Ethos* 23, no. 2 (1995): 123–48.

Arnold, David, *Police Power and Colonial Rule: Madras, 1859–1947*. Delhi: Oxford University Press, 1986.

Austin, J.L., *How To Do Things With Words* (Cambridge, MA: Harvard University Press, 1962).

Balibar Etienne, and Immanuel Wallerstein, *Race, Nation, Class: Ambiguous Identities*. (London: Verso, 1991).

Barry, Kevin, 'Critical Notes on Post-colonial Aesthetics', *Irish Studies Review* 14 (Spring 1996): 2–11.

Bartlett, Thomas, 'An End to Moral Economy: The Irish Militia Disturbances of 1793', *Past and Present* 99 (May 1983): 76–136.

—— '"What Ish My Nation?": Themes in Irish History, 1550–1850' in Thomas Bartlett et al. (eds.), *Irish Studies: A General Introduction*. Dublin: Gill & Macmillan, 1988, pp. 44–59.

Beale, Jennifer, *Women in Ireland: Voices of Change*. Bloomington: Indiana University Press, 1987.

Beames, Michael R., *Peasants and Power: The Whiteboy Movements and Their Control in Pre-Famine Ireland*. New York: 1983.

Benjamin, Walter, 'Theses on the Philosophy of History' in Hannah Arendt (ed.), *Illuminations*. Translated by Harry Zohn. New York: Schocken, 1969, pp. 253–64.

—— 'Critique of Violence' in Peter Demetz (ed.), *Reflections: Assays, Aphorisms, Autobiographical Writings*. Translated by Edmund Jephcott. New York: Harcourt Brace Jovanovich, 1978.

—— *The Origins of German Tragic Drama*. London: Verso, 1985.

—— "The Work of Art in the Age of Mechanical Reproduction" in Hannah Arendt (ed. and intro) *Illuminations*, (New York: Schocken, 1969, 219–53).

Beresford, David, *Ten Men Dead: The Story of the 1981 Irish Hunger Strike* (New York: Atlantic Monthly Press, 1987).

Bhabha, Homi, 'DissemiNation: Time, Narrative, and the Margins of the Modern Nation' in Homi Bhabha (ed.), *Nation and Narration*. London: Routledge, 1990, pp. 291–322.

—— *Locations of* Culture (London and New York: Routledge, 1994).

—— "The Other Question: Stereotype, Discrimination and the Discourse of Colonialism" in *Locations* of Culture, 66–84.

Black 47, *Fire of Freedom*. New York: SBK, 1993.

Boland, Eavan, *Outside History: Selected Poems, 1980–1990*. New York: Norton, 1990.

Bowyer Bell, J., *The Irish Troubles. A Generation of Violence, 1967–1992.* (New York: St. Martins Press, 1993).

Boylan Thomas A., and Timothy P. Foley, *Political Economy and Colonial Ireland.* (London and New York: Routledge, 1992).

Breuilly, John, *Nationalism and the State*. New York: St Martin's Press, 1982.

Butler, Judith, *Gender Trouble: Feminism and the Subversion of Identity.* (New York: Routledge, 1990).

Cahill, Liam, *Forgotten Revolution: Limerick Soviet, 1919, a Threat to British Power in Ireland.* Dublin: O'Brien Press, 1990.

Campbell, Brian, Laurence McKeown and Felim O'Hagan (eds.), *Nor Meekly Serve Our Time: The H-Block Struggle, 1976–1981*. Belfast: Beyond the Pale Publications, 1994.

Carson, Ciaran, *Belfast Confetti*. Winston-Salem: Wake Forest University Press, 1989.

Chakrabarty, Dipesh, *Rethinking Working-Class History, Bengal 1890–1940*. Princeton, NJ: Princeton University Press, 1989.

—— 'Hindu Extremism and Postmodernism: An Indian Debate on the Politics of Knowledge' (typescript).

—— 'Postcoloniality and the Artifice of History: Who Speaks for "Indian" Pasts?' *Representations* 37 (Winter 1992): 1–26.

Chandra, Bipan, 'Colonialism, Stages of Colonialism, and the Colonial State', *Journal of Contemporary Asia* 10, no. 3 (1980): 272–85.

Chatterjee, Partha, *Nationalist Thought and the Colonial World: A Derivative Discourse?* London: Zed Books, 1986.

—— *The Nation and Its Fragments: Colonial and Postcolonial Histories.* (Princeton, NJ: Princeton University Press, 1993).

Clancy, Mary, 'Aspects of Women's Contributions to the Oireachtas Debate in the Irish Free State, 1922–37' in Maria Luddy and Cliona Murphy (eds.), *Women Surviving: Studies in Irish Women's History in the 19th and 20th Centuries*. Dublin: Poolbeg, 1990, 206–32.

Clark, T. J., *The Absolute Bourgeois: Artists and Politics in France, 1848–1851*. Greenwich, CT: New York Graphic Society, 1973.

Connolly, Clara, 'Culture or Citizenship? Notes from the "Gender and Colonialism" Conference, Galway, Ireland, May 1992', *Feminist Review* 44 (Summer 1993): 104–11.

Connolly, Clara, and Pragna Patel, 'Women Who Walk on Water: Working Across "Race" in Women Against Fundamentalism' in *The Politics of Culture in the Shadow of Capitalism*. Durham, NC: Duke University Press, 1997, 388–93.

Connolly, James, *Labour in Irish History and the Reconquest of Ireland*. Dublin: Maunsel and Roberts, 1922.

Constantino, Renato, 'Identity and Consciousness: The Philippine Experience', *Journal of Contemporary Asia* 6, no. 1 (1976): 5–29.

—— *The Philippines, Vol. I: A Past Revisited*. (Manila: Privately Published, 1975).

Constantino, Renato, and Letizia Constantino, *The Philippines: The Continuing Past*. Quezon City: Foundation of Nationalist Studies, 1978.

Cooke, S. B., *Imperial Affinities: Nineteenth-Century Analogies and Exchanges between India and Ireland*. New Delhi: Sage, 1993.

Corcoran, Mary, 'New York, New York', *Irish Reporter* 1 (1st Quarter 1991): 6–9.

Coulter, Carol, *Ireland: Between the First and the Third Worlds*. (Dublin: Attic Press, 1990).

—— *The Hidden Tradition: Feminism, Women and the State in Ireland*. Cork: Cork University Press, 1993.

Crotty, Raymond, *Ireland in Crisis: A Study in Capitalist Colonial Underdevelopment*. Dingle: Brandon, 1986.

Cullen, Mary, 'History Women and History Men: The Politics of Women's History' in Daltún O'Ceallaigh (ed.), *Reconsiderations of Irish History and Culture*. Dublin: Leirmheas, 1994, pp. 113–33.

Cullen, Mary, and Maria Luddy (eds.), *Women, Power and Consciousness in Nineteenth-Century Ireland*. Dublin: Attic Press, 1995.

Curtis, Edmund, *A History of Ireland*. London: Methuen, 1961.

Curtis, Liz, *Nothing But the Same Old Story: The Roots of Anti-Irish Racism*. (London: Information on Ireland, 1984).

—— *Ireland: The Propaganda War. The British Media and the Battle for Hearts and Minds*. London: Pluto, 1984.

Davis, Mike, 'Urban Renaissance and the Spirit of Postmodernism', *New Left Review* 151 (May–June 1985): 112–13.

Deane, Seamus, *Strange Country: Modernity and Nationhood in Irish Writing since 1790*. Oxford: Oxford University Press, 1997.

Derrida, Jacques, *Margins of Philosophy*, trans. Alan Bass. (Chicago: Chicago University Press, 1982).

Dickson, D., et al. (eds.), *The United Irishmen: Republicanism, Radicalism and Rebellion*. Dublin: Lilliput, 1993.

Dirlik, Arif, 'The Postcolonial Aura: Third World Criticism in the Age of Global Capitalism', *Critical Inquiry* 20 (Winter 1994): 328–56.

Donnelly, James S., Jr, 'The Whiteboy Movement: 1761–1765', *Irish Historical Studies* 21, no. 81 (March 1978): 20–54.

Dunne, Tom, 'New Histories: Beyond "Revisionism"', *The Irish Review* 12 (Spring/Summer 1992): 1–12.

Fanon, Frantz, 'Algeria Unveiled' in *Studies in a Dying Colonialism*. Translated by Haakon Chevalier. New York: Grove Press, 1967.

—— *Black Skin, White Masks* (1952), trans. Charles Lamm Markham. (New York: Grove Press, 1967).

—— 'Racism and Culture' in *Toward the African Revolution: Political Essays*. Translated by Haakon Chevalier. New York: Grove Press, 1988.

—— *The Wretched of the Earth*. Translated by Constance Farrington. New York: Grove Press, 1963.

Feldman, Allen, *Formations of Violence: The Narrative of the Body and Political Terror in Northern Ireland*. Chicago: University of Chicago Press, 1991.

Fineman, Joel, *The Subjectivity Effect in Western Literature: Essays towards the Release of Shakespeare's Will*. Cambridge, MA: MIT Press, 1991.

Foster, R. F., *Modern Ireland, 1600–1972*. New York: Penguin, 1989.

Foucault, Michel, 'Governmentality' in Graham Burchell, Colin Gordon and Peter Miller (eds.), *The Foucault Effect: Studies in Governmentality*. London: Harvester Wheatsheaf, 1991, pp. 87–104.

Freud, Sigmund, 'The Dissolution of the Oedipal Complex' (1924) in Angela Richards (ed.), *On Sexuality: Three Essays on the Theory of Sexuality and Other Works*. Vol. 7 of The Pelican Freud. Translated by James Strachey. Harmondsworth: Penguin, 1977.

—— 'Some Psychical Consequences of the Anatomical Distinction Between the Sexes' (1925) in Angela Richards (ed.), *On Sexuality: Three Essays on the Theory of Sexuality and Other Works*. Vol. 7 of The Pelican Freud. Translated by James Strachey. Harmondsworth: Penguin, 1977.

Garvin, Thomas, *The Evolution of Irish Nationalist Politics*. Dublin: Gill & Macmillan, 1981.

Gellner, Ernest, *Nations and Nationalism*. Ithaca, NY: Cornell University Press, 1983.

Gibbons, Luke, *Transformations in Irish Culture: Allegory, History and Irish Nationalism*. Cork: Cork University Press, 1996.

Gramsci, Antonio, 'Notes on Italian History' in Quintin Hoare and Geoffrey Nowell-Smith (trans. and eds.), *Selections From the Prison Notebooks of Antonio Gramsci*. New York: International Publishers, 1971, pp. 52–120.

Gray, Peter, "Ideology and the Famine" in Cathal Portéir (ed.), *The Great Irish Famine*. (Cork: Mercier Press, 1995, 86–103).

Guerrero, Amado, 'Specific Characteristics of Our People's War' in *Philippine Society and Revolution*. 3rd edition. International Association of Filipino Patriots, 1979, pp. 179–215.

Guha, Ranajit, 'The Prose of Counter-Insurgency' in Guha and Gayatri Chakravorty Spivak (eds.), *Selected Subaltern Studies*. Oxford: Oxford University Press, 1988, pp. 45–86.

—— *A Rule of Property for Bengal: An Essay on the Idea of Permanent Settlement*. Paris: Mouton, 1963.

Guha, Ranajit, and Gayatri Chakravorty Spivak, *Selected Subaltern Studies*. Oxford: Oxford University Press, 1988.

Guinnane, Timothy W., *The Vanishing Irish: Household, Migration, and the Rural Economy, 1850–1914*. Princeton, NJ: Princeton University Press, 1997.

Gusevich, Miriam, "Decoration and Decorum": Adolf Loos's Critique of Kitsch; *New German Critique* 43 (Winter 1988), 97–123.

Guzman, Domingo Castro de, 'Millenarianism and Revolution: A Critique of Reynaldo C. Ileto's *Pasyon and Revolution*', *Journal of Social History* 3–4: 31–95.

Hall, Stuart, 'Gramsci's Relevance for the Study of Race and Ethnicity', *Journal of Communication Inquiry* 10 (Summer 1986): 5–27.

Handler, Kristin, "Sexing *The Crying Game*: Difference, Identity, Ethics", *Film Quartedy*, 47 (Spring 1994): 31–42.

Harlow, Barbara, *Barred: Women, Writing and Political Detention*. Hanover: Wesleyan University Press/University Press of New England, 1992.

Heaney, Seamus, 'Whatever You Say, Say Nothing' in *North*. London: Faber and Faber, 1975, pp. 57–60.

Hechter, Michael, *Internal Colonialism: The Celtic Fringe in British National Development, 1536–1966*. Berkeley: University of California Press, 1975.

Herr, Cheryl (ed.), *For the Land They Loved: Irish Political Melodramas, 1890–1925*. New York: Syracuse University Press, 1991.

Hill, John, "Images of Violence" in Kevin Rockett, Luke Gibbons and John Hill (eds.), *Cinema in Ireland*. (London: Routledge, 1988, 147–185).

Hillyard, Paddy, 'The Normalization of Special Powers: From Northern Ireland to Britain' in Phil Scranton (ed.), *Law, Order and the Authoritarian State: Readings in Critical Criminology*. Milton Keynes: Open University Press, 1987.

Hobsbawm, E. J., *Nations and Nationalism Since 1780: Programme, Myth and Reality*. Cambridge: Cambridge University Press, 1990.

Hussain, Nasser, 'The Jurisprudence of Emergency: Sovereignty and the Rule of Law in Colonial India'. Ph.D. dissertation, U.C. Berkeley, 1995.

Ignatiev, Noel, *How the Irish Became White*. New York, Routledge, 1997.

Ileto, Reynaldo Clemena, 'Outlines of a Non-Linear Emplotment of Philippine History' in Lisa Lowe and David Lloyd (eds.), *The Politics of Culture in the Shadow of Capitalism*. Durham, NC: Duke University Press, 1997, pp. 98–131.

—— *Pasyon and Revolution: Popular Movements in the Philippines, 1840–1910*. Manila: Ateneo de Manila, 1979.

Jameson, Fredric, Edward Said and Terry Eagleton, *Nationalism, Colonialism and Literature*. Edited by Seamus Deane. Minneapolis: University of Minnesota Press, 1990.

Jordan, Neil, *The Neil Jordan Reader*. (New York: Vintage, 1993).

Joyce, James, *Ulysses*. New York: Random House, 1986.

Kant, Immanuel, *The Conflict of the Faculties*, trans. and intro. (Mary J. Gregor. New York: Ataris, 1979).

—— 'The Idea of a Universal History on a Cosmo-Political Plan' in *Works*. Vol. 12. Translated by Thomas de Quincy. Edinburgh: Adam and Charles Black, 1862, pp. 133–52.

Kearney, Richard, and Robin Wilson, 'Northern Ireland's Future as a European Region', *Irish Review* 15 (Spring 1994): 51–69.

Kennedy, Liam, *Colonialism, Religion and Nationalism in Ireland*. Belfast: Queen's University Institute for Irish Studies, 1996.

Kiberd, Declan, *Inventing Ireland*. Cambridge, MA: Harvard University Press, 1996.

—— 'Emigration: The Same Old Story?', *Irish Reporter* 1 (1st Quarter 1991): 3–5.

—— 'Post-Colonial Ireland: "Being Different"' in Daltún O'Ceallaigh (ed.), *Reconsiderations of Irish History and Culture*. Dublin: Leirmheas, 1994, pp. 94–112.

Kitson, Brigadier Frank, *Low Intensity Operations: Subversion, Insurgency and Peace-Keeping*. London: Faber, 1971.

—— *Bunch of Five*. London: Faber and Faber, 1977.

Lloyd, David, *Anomalous States: Irish Writing and the Post-Colonial Moment*. Dublin: Lilliput Press, 1993.

—— *Nationalism and Minor Literature: James Clarence Mangan and the Emergence of Irish Cultural Nationalism*. Berkeley: University of California Press, 1987.

Lloyd David, and Paul Thomas, *Culture and the State*. (New York and London: Routledge, 1997).

Lowe, Lisa, *Immigrant Acts: On Asian American Cultural Politics*. (Duke University Press, 1996).

Lorimer, Norman, 'Philippine Communism: An Historical Overview', *Journal of Contemporary Asia* 7, no. 4 (1977): 462–85.

Lowe, Lisa, *Critical Terrains: British and French Orientalisms*. Ithaca, NY: Cornell University Press, 1991.

Lowe, Lisa, and David Lloyd (eds.), *The Politics of Culture in the Shadow of Capital*. Durham, NC: Duke University Press, 1997.

Lucero, Rosario Cruz, *Negros Occidental, 1970–1986: The Fall of the Sugar Industry and the Rise of the People's Theater*. Ph.D. dissertation, University of the Philippines, 1990.

Luddy, Maria, and Cliona Murphy (eds.), *Women Surviving: Studies in Irish Women's History in the 19th and 20th Centuries*. Dublin: Poolbeg, 1990.

Lugowski, David, "Genre Conventions and Visual Style in *The Crying Game*", *Cineaste* 20.1 (1993): 31.

Lukacs, Georg, *The Theory of the Novel*, Trans. Anna Bostock. (Cambridge, MA: MIT Press, 1971).

Lustick, Ian, *Unsettled States, Disputed Lands: Britain and Ireland, France and Algeria, Israel and the West Bank–Gaza*. Ithaca, NY: Cornell University Press, 1993.

Lyons, F. S. L., *Ireland since the Famine*. London: Weidenfeld and Nicolson, 1971.

McAliskey, Bernadette Devlin, 'Where Are We Now in the Peace Process?' *Irish Reporter* 21 (February 1996): 23–8.

McCartney, Donald, 'History Revisions: Good and Bad' in Daltún O'Ceallaigh (ed.), *Reconsiderations of Irish History and Culture*. Dublin: Leirmheas, 1994, 134–56.

McClintock, Anne, 'The Angel of Progress: Pitfalls of the Term "Post-Colonialism"', *Social Text* 31/32 (1992).

MacCurtain, Margaret, and Donncha Ó Corrain (eds.), *Women in Irish Society: The Historical Dimension*. Westport, CT: Greenwood Press, 1979.

MacLaughlin, Jim, 'Ireland: An "Emigrant Nursery" in the World Economy', *International Quarterly Review* 31, no. 1 (1993): 149–70.

—— 'Place, Politics, and Culture in Nation-Building Ulster: Constructing Nationalist Hegemony in Post-Famine Donegal', *Canadian Review of Studies in Nationalism* 20, no. 1–2 (1993): 97–111.

—— 'Social Characteristics and Destination of Recent Emigrants from Selected Regions in the West of Ireland', *Geoforum* 22, no. 3 (1991): 319–31.

MacSiomoin, Tomas, 'The Colonized Mind: Irish Language and Society' in Daltún O'Ceallaigh (ed.), *Reconsiderations of Irish History and Culture*. Dublin: Leirmeas, pp. 42–71.

Markievicz, Constance, *Prison Letters*. London: Longman, 1934.

Marx, Karl, *A Contribution to the Critique of Political Economy*. Edited by Maurice Dobb. Translated by S. W. Ryazanskaya. Moscow: Progress Publishers, 1970.

—— 'On the Jewish Question' in *Early Writings*. Translated by Rodney Livingstone and Gregor Benton. New York: Vintage, 1974, 211–42.

—— A Contribution to the Critique of Political Economy. Edited by Maurice Dobb. Translated by S. W. Ryazanskaya. Moscow: Progress Publishers, 1970.

Marxman, 33 Revolutions per Minute. London: Phonogram, 1993.

Michel, Frann, "Racial and Sexual Politics in The Crying Game", Cineaste 20.1 (1993): 30.

Miller, Kerby, Emigrants and Exiles. Oxford: Oxford University Press, 1985.

Mitter, Swasti, Common Fate, Common Bond. London: Pluto Press, 1986.

Mohanty, Chandra T., 'Cartographies of Struggle: Third World Women and the Politics of Feminism' in Chandra Talpade Mohanty, Ann Russo and Lourdes Torres (eds.), Third World Women and the Politics of Feminism. Bloomington: Indiana University Press, 1991, pp. 1–47.

—— "Under Western Eyes" in Third World Women and the Politics of Feminism, ed. CTM, Ann Russo and Lourdes Torres. (Bloomington: Indiana University Press, 1991, pp. 51–80).

Mommsen, Wolfgang T., Theories of Imperialism, trans. P. S. Falla. New York: Random House, 1980.

Moraga, Cherrie, "A Long Line of Vendidas", in Loving in the War Years. (Boston: South End Press, 1983).

Moretti, Franco, The Way of the World. (London: Verso, 1987).

Murphy, Cliona, 'Women's History, Feminist History, or Gender History?', The Irish Review 12 (Spring/Summer 1992): 21–6.

Nairn, Tom, The Break-up of Britain: Crisis and Neo-Nationalism. London: New Left Books, 1977.

Nandy, Ashis, The Intimate Enemy: Loss and Recovery of Self Under Colonialism. (Delhi: Oxford University Press, 1983).

Ní Dhonnchadha, Mairín, and Theo Dorgan (eds.), Revising the Rising. Derry: Field Day, 1991.

Norman, Diana, Terrible Beauty: The Life of Constance Markievicz. Dublin: Poolbeg, 1991.

O'Ceallaigh, Daltún (ed.), Reconsiderations of Irish History and Culture. Dublin: Leirmheas, 1994.

O'Connor, Emmet, Syndicalism in Ireland, 1917–1923. Cork: Cork University Press, 1988.

O'Hearn, Denis, "The Celtic Tiger: The Role of the Multi-Nationals" in Jim MacLaughlin and Ethel Crowley, Under the Belly of the Tiger: Class, Race, Identity and Culture in the Global Ireland. (Dublin: Irish Reporter Publications, 1997).

Olalquiaga, Celeste, Megalopolis: Contemporary Cultural Sensibilities. Minnesota: University of Minnesota Press, 1992.

O'Neill, James W., 'A Look at Captain Rock: Agrarian Rebellion in Ireland, 1815–1845', Eire–Ireland 17, no. 1 (Autumn 1982): 17–34.

Patajo-Legasto, Priscelina, Philippine Contemporary Theater, 1946–1985: A Materialist Analysis. Ph.D. dissertation, University of the Philippines, 1988.

Radhakrishnan, R., 'Nationalism, Gender and the Narrative of Identity' in Andrew Parker, Mary Russo, Doris Sommer and Patricia Yaeger (eds.), Nationalisms and Sexualities. New York: Routledge, 1992.

Ransom, Bernard, Connolly's Marxism. (London: Pluto, 1980).

Regan, Colm, 'Latin American Dependency Theory and its Relevance to Ireland', The Crane Bag 6, no. 2 (1982): 15–20.

Rockett, Kevin, "Disguising Dependence: Separatism and Foreign Mass Culture", *Circa* 49 (Jan/Feb 1990): 20–5

Roediger, David, *The Wages of Whiteness: Race and the Making of the American Working Class.* London: Verso, 1991.

Rolston, Bill, *Drawing Support: Murals in Northern Ireland.* Belfast: Beyond the Pale, 1992.

—— 'The Writing on the Wall: The Murals of Gerry Kelly', *Irish Reporter* 2 (2nd Quarter 1991): 14–17.

Ross, John, *Rebellion from the Roots: Indian Uprisings in Chiapas.* Monroe, ME: Common Courage Press, 1995.

Ruane, Catriona, 'A Memoir of Development', *Irish Reporter* 12 (4th Quarter 1993): 19–20.

Ryan, William, *The Irish Labour Movement.* (Dublin: Talbot Press, 1919).

Said, Edward, *Orientalism.* (New York: Vintage, 1979).

Sangari, KumKum, 'Relating Histories: Definitions of Literacy, Literature, Gender in Early Nineteenth Century Calcutta and England' in Srati Joshi (ed.), *Rethinking English: Essays in Literature, Language, History.* (New Delhi: Trianka, 1991, 32–123).

—— *Recasting Women: Essays in Indian Colonial History.* New Delhi: Kali for Women, 1989.

Scott, Andrew M., *Insurgency.* Chapel Hill: University of North Carolina Press, 1970.

Shohat, Ella, 'Notes on the "Post-Colonial"', *Social Text* 31/32 (1992): 99–113.

Simpson, Mark, *Male Impersonators: Men Performing Masculinity.* (London: Cassell, 1994).

Smyth, Jim, *The Men of No Property: Irish Radicals and Popular Politics in the Late Eighteenth Century.* London: Macmillan, 1992.

Spivak, Gayatri Chakravorty, 'Deconstructing Historiography' in Ranajit Guha and Spivak (eds.), *Selected Subaltern Studies.* Oxford: Oxford University Press, 1988, pp. 3–52.

Stewart, A. T. Q., *The Narrow Ground: The Roots of Conflict in Ulster.* Revised edition. London: Faber and Faber, 1989.

—— 'A Scholar and a Gentleman' (interview with Hiram Morgan), *History Ireland* (Summer 1993): 55–8.

Thompson, E. P., 'The Moral Economy of the English Crowd in the Eighteenth Century', *Past and Present* 50 (February 1971): 76–136.

Todd, Jennifer, 'The Limits of Britishness', *Irish Review* 5 (Autumn 1988): 11–16.

Torres-Reyes, Lulu, 'Anticipating Hegemony: Brecht and the Philippines Today', *Makisa* 1, no. 1 (1st Quarter, 1989): 18–19.

Townsend, Charles, *Political Violence in Ireland: Government and Resistance since 1848.* (Oxford: Oxford University Press, 1983).

Valiulis, Maryann Gialanella, and Mary O'Dowd (eds.), *Women and Irish Women History: Essays in Honour of Margaret MacCurtain.* Dublin: Wolfhound Press, 1997.

Viswenathan, Gauri, *Masks of Conquest: Literary Study and British Rule in India.* (New York: Columbia University Press, 1989).

Ward, Margaret, *Maud Gonne: Ireland's Joan of Arc.* London: Pandora, 1990.

Whelan, Kevin, 'Come All Ye Blinkered Nationalists: A Post-Revisionist Agenda for Irish History', *Irish Reporter* 2 (2nd Quarter 1991): 24–6.

—— 'The Power of Place', *The Irish Review* 12 (Spring/Summer 1992): 13–20.

—— The Tree of Liberty: Radicalism, Catholicism and the Construction of Irish Identity, 1760–1830. Cork: Cork University Press, 1996.

Williams, Patrick, and Laura Chrisman (eds.), Colonial Discourse and Post-colonial Theory. New York: Columbia University Press, 1994.

Williams, Raymond, The Country and the City. New York: Oxford University Press, 1973.

—— Marxism and Literature. Oxford: Oxford University Press, 1977.

Wright, Steve, 'An Assessment of the New Technologies of Repression' in Marjo Hoefnagels (ed.), Repression and Repressive Violence. Amsterdam: Swets & Zeitlinger, 1977.

Yadav, Alok, 'Nationalism and Contemporaneity: Political Economy of a Discourse', Cultural Critique 26 (Winter 1993–4): 191–229.

Ziff, Trisha, Distant Relations: Chicano, Irish, Mexican Art and Critical Writing, ed. Trisha Ziff. (New York: Smart Art Press, 1996).

INDEX

abortion legislation, 86
Adams, Gerry, 4
Adorno, Theodor, 34, 91
aesthetics, 63–4
Africa, 20
African American culture, 101–2
agrarian movements, 15–16, 44–5, 55, 83, 84, 114n
agriculture in Ireland, 10, 44
  emergence of farming class, 85, 103
Aguinaldo, Emilio, 30
Algeria, 8
Althusser, Louis, 34, 35
Anderson, Benedict, 19, 26, 90
Anglo-Irish war (1919–22), 28
Archer, Ann, 72–3
Aristotle
  Poetics, 63
Arnold, Matthew
  Culture and Anarchy, 56

ballads, 83, 89, 90, 103, 125n
Barry, Kevin
  'Critical Notes on Postcolonial Aesthetics', 15
Barthes, Roland
  Elements of Semiology, 54
Bartlett, Thomas, 15
  '"What Ish My Nation?"', 5–7
Belfast, 46, 48, 49, 51, 104
  murals, 94–5
Benjamin, Walter, 1, 25, 27, 84, 98
materialist historiography, 41–2, 43
Bentham, Jeremy
  Panopticon, 51
Bhabha, Homi, 61
Blanqui, Louis, 41
Bonifacio, Andres, 30
Bowyer Bell, J.
  The Irish Troubles, 53–4, 55, 57, 59
Boylan, Thomas, 16
Breuilly, John, 19
Britain
  and agrarian movement, 45
  counter-insurgency techniques, 46–9, 62–3, 65, 67, 106, 117n

colonialism of, 9–11, 14–15, 54, 55, 79
  industrialization, 10
  Irish emigration policy, 11
  racism, 64, 65, 104, 115n
British Army, 46

Camnitzer, Luis, 104
capitalism, 1, 4, 14, 40, 107
  alienating effects, 92
  and gender relations, 86, 88
Caribbean, 15, 101
Carson, Ciaran
  Belfast Confetti, 49–52
Catholicism, 103
celtic mythology, 87, 94, 95
Chakrabarty, Dipesh, 16
Chatterjee, Partha, 16, 40
cinematic conventions, 67
Civil Rights Movement, 47
Close, Glenn, 72–3
colonialism, 2–14, 29, 58–9
  abstraction, 14
  comparative work on studies of, 15–16
  definition of, 6–7
  differential analysis, 3, 14–15, 16
  Ghana and India compared to Ireland, 10–11
  and hybridity, 44, 46
  and Irish resistance to modernization, 8
  and mixing of cultural forms, 89
  and myth, 76
  in Philippines, 30
  and racism, 6, 22, 104–6
  state violence, 3–4, 10, 47–9, 54–5, 60, 62
  trade and, 10–11
  in United States, 6–7, 14, 15
  see also postcolonial projects; subalternity
Communist Party of the Philippines (CPP), 29–30
  'conscientization', 31, 44
Connolly, Clara, 86–7
Connolly, James, 9, 10, 16, 28, 40, 98, 99
Constantino, Renato, 24
Corcoran, Mary, 102
counter-insurgency techniques, 46–9, 62–3, 65, 67, 95, 117n